What People Are Say

Chicken Soup for the Priso...

"*Chicken Soup for the Prisoner's Soul* brought out feelings and emotions I forgot I had. It had a positive influence on me and helped give me a sense of hope, self-esteem and empowerment in finding new ways to live successfully."

Edward Smith
inmate

"As a wife of an incarcerated man, I found strength in the human race. When this part of my life started, I never thought I would make it through this. These stories from these authors show inmates are still humans. *Chicken Soup for the Prisoner's Soul* helped me feel like there is still hope for the future."

Jennifer Skaggs
an inmate's wife

"The heartwarming stories in *Chicken Soup for the Prisoner's Soul* put faces on those who are incarcerated, their loved ones and those who minister to them. Their positive strides as illustrated in this book will touch the reader and linger long after the last page is turned."

Lana Robertson Hayes
educator

"Gripping insight into the triumphant spirit of the human soul in the most dismal of circumstances. These uplifting stories remind me of many inmates I met and dealt with during my father's twenty-year tenure as a warden. I heartily endorse this book for all readers."

William J. Buchanan
author of *Execution Eve*

"Reading these stories has reinforced my belief that there is a part within every one of us which delights in contributing to the spiritual well-being of others."

Allen Nagy, Ph.D.
mental health professional
author, *How to Raise Your Child's Emotional Intelligence*

"These stories filled my heart with love. *Chicken Soup for the Prisoner's Soul* helps people in the mainstream realize that there are also good people inside prison."

Frank Milano
prisoner

"There is much to be learned from these stories of adversity and from the growth that comes from working through pain. For those of us lucky enough to not know such suffering first-hand, these testimonials are a great gift."

Susan Sarandon
Academy Award-winner
(Dead Man Walking)

"*Chicken Soup for the Prisoner's Soul* provides that essential element of hope that is so needed by all of our free and non-free souls."

J. Michael Quinlan
president, Corrections Corporation of America
former director, Federal Bureau of Prisons

"This book should be in every cell nationwide. It is sure to heal hearts and uplift spirits, as well as offer important practical guidance to prisoners everywhere. Thank you for putting together this invaluable resource."

Robin Casarjian
author, *Houses of Healing: A Prisoner's Guide to Inner Power and Freedom*

"Through these moving and entertaining stories, we are given clear pictures of how lives are changed and redirected toward success and fulfillment."

Grady Jim Robinson
speaker and author, *Did I Ever Tell You About the Time?*

"While reading a story from this book to my ninth-grade at-risk youths, our vice-principal unexpectedly stepped into the classroom for a brief visit. Later she said, 'I was stunned at how quiet the students were for you.' I said, 'Ann, they were quiet because they were listening to a letter from a father they all wished they had.'"

Sue Billington-Wade
educator

"This book should be required reading for all high school students. I also encourage every teacher to read this book as a way of showing that they too can make a difference in the lives of their students."

Ernie Savage
director of chapel ministries
Okinawa, Japan

"These stories make people wake up and see that people incarcerated are human beings with feelings . . . and not just *convicts*."

Cindy Wilhite
loved one

"This book, along with good programs in our prison systems, can be a ripple toward the healing of the soul."

Cata Low
Avatar trainer

"It is of utmost importance to remember prison inmates as sons and daughters, fathers and mothers, uncles and aunts."

Rev. Hugh J. Daley
chaplain

"*Chicken Soup for the Prisoner's Soul* shares a nourishing recipe of support and insightful reflection. Reading this book is time well spent. The best thing is you do not have to be in jail to enjoy it. Violence ends where love begins. Join in the Cell-Liberation and share it with a friend."

Tom Duffy
executive program director
Prison SMART Foundation Incorporated

"By reading these stories, we can gain the insight and knowledge necessary to learn more about not only prison inmates who are often not forgiven, but about ourselves."

Kim Raiani
volunteer who visits death-row inmates

"*Chicken Soup for the Prisoner's Soul* is a warm collection of testimonials that speak to the good in each of us and remind us of our membership in the human family."

Jim Mustin
president, Family and Corrections Network

"*Chicken Soup for the Prisoner's Soul* gives voices to the men, women and children incarcerated in silence. Its mere presence in the public eye is a conscious wake-up call that prisoners do have souls."

Penny Rayfield
founder, C-Cubed Institute

"This book helps all those involved with someone who has been incarcerated to keep their vision of faith and success."

Elizabeth Sabo
Designing Success

CHICKEN SOUP
FOR THE
PRISONER'S SOUL

Chicken Soup for the Prisoner's Soul
101 Stories to Open the Heart and Rekindle the Spirit of Hope, Healing and Forgiveness
Jack Canfield, Mark Victor Hansen, Tom Lagana

Published by Backlist, LLC,
a unit of Chicken Soup for the Soul Publishing, LLC. www.chickensoup.com

Front cover redesign by Larissa Hise
Originally published in 2000 by Health Communications, Inc.

Back cover and spine redesign by Pneuma Books, LLC

Distributed to the booktrade by Simon & Schuster. SAN: 200-2442

Publisher's Cataloging-in-Publication Data
(Prepared by The Donohue Group)

Chicken soup for the prisoner's soul : 101 stories to open the heart and rekindle the spirit of hope, healing and forgiveness / [compiled by] Jack Canfield, Mark Victor Hansen, [and] Tom Lagana.

p. : ill. ; cm.

Originally published: Deerfield Beach, FL : Health Communications, c2000.
ISBN: 978-1-62361-096-8

1. Prisoners--Conduct of life--Anecdotes. 2. Prisoners--Education--Anecdotes. 3. Moral education--Anecdotes. 4. Spiritual life--Anecdotes. 5. Anecdotes. I. Canfield, Jack, 1944- II. Hansen, Mark Victor. III. Lagana, Tom, 1944-

HV8869 .C56 2012
248.8/6   2012944869

PRINTED IN THE UNITED STATES OF AMERICA
on acid free paper

CHICKEN SOUP
FOR THE
PRISONER'S SOUL

101 Stories to Open the Heart and Rekindle the Spirit of Hope, Healing and Forgiveness

Jack Canfield
Mark Victor Hansen
Tom Lagana

Backlist, LLC, a unit of
Chicken Soup for the Soul Publishing, LLC
Cos Cob, CT
www.chickensoup.com

Contents

2. ON CHANGE

3. ON FAITH

6. ON LOVE

7. OVERCOMING OBSTACLES

8. ON WISDOM

How This Book Came to Be

Never doubt that a small group of thoughtful, committed citizens can change the world. Indeed, it is the only thing that ever has.

Margaret Mead

During my engineering career, I joined Toastmasters International to improve my public speaking abilities. In June 1992, I brought their magazine to read on a business trip. It was an evening flight with few passengers aboard, and the cabin lights were out. Midway through the flight, I began to read an article, "Walking Tall in Toastmasters," that deeply touched my soul and changed my life forever. An inmate from Oklahoma, Rex Moore Jr., wrote the article. By the end of his story, tears streamed down my face. I whispered to myself, "Wow!"

I decided to write to the author immediately. I pulled out a pad of lined paper and wrote Rex a short note followed by a letter to the editor of the magazine.

About a week later, Rex responded with a touching letter and thanked me for my comments. My letter appeared in the September 1992 issue. At the end of the letter, I mentioned that some day I looked forward to attending a meeting in prison. I don't know why I even said that; after all I had absolutely no connections to inmates or prison work.

Totally unrelated to Rex's article and my letter, Toastmasters headquarters in California had received two letters from an inmate, Robert Squeeky Saunders, who requested that a prison club be started in Delaware, and no one had responded yet. Our regional representative approached me and said, "I have a letter for you to answer. You don't have to go to the prison—just answer the letter." I sent the inmate a note right away.

A few weeks later, I received a call from program coordinator Fran Cockroft at Gander Hill Prison. She requested that I go to the prison and explain the Toastmasters' program to the inmates and prison staff. I recruited five others to assist me and scheduled a demonstration meeting for mid-December 1992. The prison happened to be only a mile from my office. Was this a coincidence?

Six of us conducted a meeting for this project we called "Walking Tall Toastmasters," based on the title of Rex's inspiring article. More than fifty inmates and several staff members attended our first meeting, and our weekly program was born. In March 1993, we chartered the group with thirty-six dedicated members.

This was a major milestone in many of our lives—getting to know some people who would ordinarily be labeled as worthless. Why did these men want to join our group? Was it just an opportunity to socialize with people from the outside? Some of these men had a sincere desire to change. Inmates have the opportunity to speak to the parole board. Others addressed youth in an attempt to persuade them not to make the same mistakes they did. Fellow inmates taught others to help them earn their GEDs, break compulsive behaviors, find alternatives to violence, prepare for release and spread the word of God. These men took positive steps to become effective communicators.

The inmates who attended our meetings were involved in other prison programs, and I received many requests to present seminars and mentor inmates throughout the prison.

In early 1995, I was downsized after more than thirty years with one corporation. I took another engineering position and realized it was time to do something else in life. Thanks to my speaking experience I fulfilled a goal to become a Seminar Leader. I began working part time in my engineering job in September 1996 and became an independent trainer.

The warden at Gander Hill Prison asked me to present a series of seminars for a group of one hundred men in the spring of 1997. These inmates didn't have an existing program and would be released soon. Over an eight-week period, I scheduled the prison seminars between my part-time engineering job and public seminars. I went to a bookstore in search of resources to inspire the inmates. I noticed books similar to the *Chicken Soup for the Soul* series and decided to start my own book of touching stories about inmates.

During these eight weeks, my engineering project ended, and I was downsized a second time. Before the prison seminars were completed, I had the opportunity to attend Jack Canfield's eight-day Facilitation Skills Seminar (FSS) in Santa Barbara, California. During one of the breaks, I asked Jack for some advice about working with the prison population. Then I told him I had started a *Chicken Soup*-type book of stories for inmates. Jack said, "Mark and I have been talking about putting together a *Chicken Soup for the Prisoner's Soul* book, but we don't have anyone who is willing to own the project."

I didn't know what "owning" the project meant, but

that didn't matter. I quickly said, "Well, *I* will. What do I need to do?"

Jack told me to write him a note, and he would contact me after the seminar. The next morning, I gave Jack a brief note (from my pad of lined paper) that simply reminded him of our conversation and my interest in "owning" the project. A week after FSS, I received a letter from Jack Canfield on *Chicken Soup for the Soul* letterhead stating that he and Mark Victor Hansen would love for me to do this project with them.

For nearly three years, we wrote, collected, edited and had more than five hundred stories (out of the six thousand submitted) scored by a diverse group of reviewers from across the world. We have written to thousands of inmates, ex-inmates, their loved ones, prison staff, prison volunteers and victims of crime. Almost every morning after breakfast, my wife, Laura, and I lingered at the kitchen table for half an hour longer. While she read the newspaper in search of prison-related stories, people and organizations, I read the new stories that arrived and wrote to inmates.

In January 1999, we had enough highly-rated stories to place the project on "the front burner." We obtained permissions from the contributing authors and edited the best stories to send to forty reviewers across the world in April 1999. Our final reviewers included inmates and ex-inmates, their respective loved ones, prison staff and volunteers, a judge, an ex-senator, and victims of crime. As new stories arrived, they made their way through the same process until the final selection and editing in January 2000.

We are committed to putting this book into the hands of all prisoners in the U.S. and hopefully in many other parts of the world. Our goal is to make a significant difference in the lives of millions of people to nourish hope, promote healing and facilitate forgiveness. We thank you and appreciate you for being a part of this process.

Tom Lagana

Introduction

From our hearts to yours, we are delighted to offer you *Chicken Soup for the Prisoner's Soul.* This book contains stories that we know will inspire and motivate you to love more fully and unconditionally, live with more passion and compassion, and pursue your heartfelt dreams with greater conviction, bolder action and stronger perseverance.

Everyone has a story. No matter what we do for a living, how much we have in our bank account or our skin color, we have a story. Each one of us has a story, whether it is visible to the eye or locked inside us. We are encouraged to believe that our past, our circumstances, both physical and emotional, and our experiences are that story. Our mental picture of our life's story encompasses what we perceive to be true about ourselves and our possibilities.

The life one is born into is not necessarily our destiny. All of us have the power to rewrite our story, to recast the drama of our lives and to redirect the actions of the main character—ourselves. The outcomes of our lives are determined mainly by our responses to each event. Do we choose to be the hero or victim in our life's drama?

Good stories, like the best mentors in our lives, are door openers. They are unique experiences containing insights tied to emotional triggers that get our attention and stay in our memories. These stories can free us from being bound to decisions of the past and open us to understanding ourselves and to the opportunities that present themselves. A really good story allows us to recognize the choices that are open to us and see new alternatives we might never have seen before. It can give us permission to try (or at least consider trying) a new path of action.

Many of the people you will meet in these pages provide a model of unconditional acts of kindness and love. You will find great courage and foresight, belief when cynicism would be the norm, a sense of hope in what the world has to offer, and the inspiration to seek that hope for ourselves.

Some of the stories you will refer to again and again because the message is one of comfort and encouragement. Other stories will inspire you to share them with your family, friends and associates.

Here is what one of our initial reviewers wrote after reading the manuscript:

> *I just wanted to thank you for allowing me to be a reader for the* Chicken Soup for the Prisoner's Soul *book. It has been a wonderful, uplifting experience.*
>
> *I personally do not know anyone who is in prison. I can only try to imagine what those who are incarcerated, their families and their friends must be going through. The stories have made me take a closer look at their lives and my own. It seems there is hope in a hopeless place. It seems there is activity in a place where there might not be. It seems there is growth in a place where there isn't any room to grow.*
>
> *Over the past several months, my personal introspection has given me some doubts with respect to my religious faith. I have questioned the importance of God and faith to a limited extent. However, that has all*

changed . . . with many of the stories in the book about people who have used religion to better themselves, to make sense of their world and to get through years of incarceration.

Couple the book with the reports and interviews with family members of the students murdered in Littleton, Colorado, as they talk about God's purpose, faith, family, hope and forgiveness. Both have strengthened my beliefs in my religion.

In closing, thank you for the experience; it has helped me more than you can ever know!

Take care,

Neil S. Bagadiong

We believe that this book will sustain you during times of challenge, frustration and failure, and comfort you during times of confusion, pain and loss. We hope it will truly become a lifelong companion, offering continual insight and wisdom in many areas of your life.

How to Read This Book

We have been blessed with readers from all over the world who have given us feedback. We've been particularly touched by those readers who have reconnected to loved ones or old friends as a result of being inspired by one of the stories.

Some people choose to read our books from cover to cover, others pick out a particular chapter that interests them. Most people tell us that they find it works best to read one or two stories at a time, and really savor the feelings and lessons that the stories evoke. Some people read one story out loud before or after a meal with their families. Others tell us they begin their team meetings with a story selected and read by an inmate or staffperson. Our advice is to take your time and really let each story affect you at a deep level. Ask yourself how you could apply the lessons learned to your own life.

Engage each story as if it mattered, as if it could make a real difference in your life. Some have told us they keep their *Chicken Soup* book at their bedside, reading one story each night, often rereading favorites.

Many times we have been approached by readers—at a presentation or seminar—who have told us how one or more stories were most valuable to them during a period of trial and testing, such as their feeling of hopelessness, the death of a loved one or a serious illness. We are grateful for having had the opportunity to be of help to so many people in this way.

Compiling these stories has taken a lot of work, and we feel we have selected 101 gems. We hope you will love these stories as we have loved them. May they bring you hope, forgiveness, laughter, insight, healing and empowerment.

We hope that we can, in a small way, contribute to your life by bringing you these models of ordinary people doing extraordinary things to guide you on your journey. We wish that, in the pages of this book, there is a story that holds the key to doors that need opening in your life.

You may choose the path of readers who have gone before you, or simply enjoy reading this book with no particular pattern in mind, letting each story guide your thoughts and your directions. Find the path that's best for you, and most of all, enjoy!

Every day I have an opportunity to make a positive difference in someone's life. It could be by a simple smile, a reassuring glance, or a kind word. And it may be with someone I don't know.

Kathleen Gage
Message of Hope

1

ON FAMILY

The family is our refuge and springboard; nourished on it, we can advance to new horizons.

Alex Haley

Even the Strong Have a Soft Spot

Reading is to the mind what exercise is to the body.

Sir Richard Steele

When I arrived at Folsom Prison fifteen years ago, I was so much of a fish (slang for new prisoner) that I swear scales used to fall off of me as I walked. So I didn't know any better when I had my first encounter with one of the more respected prisoners whom everyone called Scat Cat.

He lived only a few doors down the tier from my cell, and each time I saw him I would be friendly and tell him "Hello." At first the man paid no attention to me, but after several days, he began to acknowledge and accept my new presence in his world by returning the salutations I offered.

Three weeks passed, when one day as I was making my way back to my cell, I found an envelope on the floor of the tier. Stopping, I picked up the wrinkled, dog-eared piece of mail and read the address. The name on the front didn't strike a chord, but the cell number written on it did.

Hesitantly I walked over to Scat Cat's cell. He was sitting on his bunk, the top half of his body bent over a makeshift table. Stone-faced, he concentrated on what he was doing.

Unsure as to whether or not to interrupt him, I decided to press forward. "Scat Cat," I called.

He responded with a look that resembled more of an annoyance than curiosity. I slid the envelope up onto the bars of his cell. "I found this on the floor."

Leaping up, Scat Cat snatched the envelope off the bars, reminding me of a lion pouncing on a piece of meat. "Did you read it?" he growled, while holding the letter protectively in his hands.

I assured him I hadn't and busied myself with looking at the various pieces of artwork that lined his cell walls. Changing the subject, I began complimenting him on the drawings.

Off-guard now, Scat Cat eased up a little. He told me he had done the work and showed me the picture he had been busy with when I interrupted him. It was a beautiful collage of bits of prison life melding into a scenic view of the outside world.

Somehow we buried ourselves in conversation, and we found we each had so much in common with the other. We must have spoken for half an hour straight, and would have continued except that the floor cop came by and chased me back to my cell.

The next day when I went outside, I eyed Scat Cat sitting alone at one of the cement tables that dotted the yard. He signaled for me to join him, and I made my way over.

After sitting down we spoke for a while, when I noticed his hand slide underneath the table out of sight. Not knowing what to think, I tried to remain calm. I had no idea what he was reaching for. It crossed my mind that maybe it was a shank, but I couldn't think of anything I had done to offend Scat Cat, so I hopefully pushed that thought out of my mind.

Imagine my surprise when he pulled his hand back up and placed the envelope I had found on the tier onto the table. He looked at me as if attempting to determine his next step. Then almost shyly, this proud man explained to me that he had received the letter, but that he could not read.

At first I didn't comprehend the meaning of his words. He sat there with his granite stare, eyeing me. Then out of nowhere, "I'll read it to you if you want me to" popped out of my mouth.

Without a word Scat Cat pushed the envelope closer to me. I picked it up and pulled the letter out. Unfolding it, I looked at the date it bore and took note that the letter was three months old. A quick peek at the postmark on the front of the envelope confirmed the fact, and I realized that Scat Cat must have been carrying this letter with him for all that time.

The letter was from his daughter, and as I read it Scat Cat's face softened with each word I relayed. Soon he was sitting with an ear-to-ear smile.

In that instant I realized just how powerful love is. It had transcended the miles, endured the distance of time and come to rest in this man's heart. I spent the rest of that yard time rereading the letter to my new friend as he shared stories with me about his daughter.

Later he did a drawing for her. Having found out that he hadn't seen the girl in eight years, I took it upon myself to write a short poem for him to give her, carefully choosing words I believed he felt for her. It may have been the lighting, but I thought I spotted a tear as I read it to him.

I may never find out what she thought of these things Scat Cat sent, because he was transferred to another prison before receiving a reply. But I like to think that his daughter was as happy to hear from her father as he was to hear from her.

I didn't ask Scat Cat what possessed him to open his world to a guy who had just fallen off the bus, but the reason really isn't important. What mattered was that within the land behind the walls, two men found an odd thing—trust.

Since then, I cherish every letter I receive even more. It's so easy to take our loved ones for granted. I saw, in Scat Cat's case, words from friends and family are what help keep the torch of the soul afire with hope and life. I pass this message on to others every day.

Robert Fuentes

The Sunray Catcher

Sometimes the heart sees what is invisible to the eye.

H. Jackson Brown Jr.

Today, in the prison chow hall, I overheard a young female officer talking to another officer. She was talking about her special little girl. Seems this little girl was standing on the front seat of her car the other day, grabbing at the sunrays as they reflected off the windshield. When her mother asked her what she was doing, the little girl said she was trying to catch a sunray for her mom as a present. Both officers agreed on how special moments like that were. The other officer then asked if this mother got to spend time with her special little girl.

"No, but when my career gets back on track, I'll have more time to spend with her, when she is older," said the young mother.

I wanted to scream and tell that mother to spend every single second she possibly can with her child, but I couldn't. Maybe after you read what follows, you will better understand.

It's the awful truth, as it happened to me. It starts with an unwritten letter—a letter I can never send:

Dear Kent,

As I look at you, I see your hair is nicely combed. I remember the hours and gallons of water we used, trying to train your hair. It always seemed to have a mind of its own. I can see that scar on your lip; hardly shows now, too. We were worried about that. You were such a brave little man when I took you to Dr. Nordquist to get those three stitches in it. I was the one who almost fainted when they started sticking you with that needle. The nurse even made me leave the room.

On the way home, I told you that you could have any treat you wanted, for being so brave. You wanted a cup of coffee, "Like big men drink," you said. My five-year-old little brave man, drinking coffee in the Rainbow Restaurant, just like big men. It was our secret; lucky Mom never found out, huh?

You have grown tall and nice looking. Grandpa always said you were going to be a big man. Guess what I'm proudest of in you? It's your kindness to all things. When we found out that your little dog, Porkchop, was epileptic, you were so happy that you cried. You had seen Porkchop have fits many times, and we were sure he would die. For three years after that, you faithfully gave Porkchop his pill every day.

I remember the day you helped me fix my pickup. We sure got greasy—Mom wouldn't even let us in the house for lunch, but we fooled her. We went to the store and got a pizza, then lipped off to Mom and your two brothers, while eating it, still dirty. Yes, that was fun. We laughed a lot that day. I found out later that you did save a piece of pizza for your little brother; it was our secret too.

I've always been proud of you for so many reasons, Kent. Your silent kindness and strength, your loyalty, your soft heart and secrets you shared with me. I remember how you used to lay across my lap with your shirt pulled up, exposing your bare back. I would trace my fingers lightly over your skin; it seemed to almost hypnotize you. I had done it many times when you were a baby, to get you to sleep when you weren't feeling good. Guess you just never grew out of liking it. I liked it too.

I remember the day I came to tell you that I was going away for a long time—going to prison. You stood silently, listening with your head bowed and tears in your eyes, asking why. You hugged me and ran up into the woods, to your secret fort, crying. I cried too that day, Kent. I was ashamed of myself, and of breaking your heart.

You did write me and send the colored pictures you drew in school. I had them on my cell wall for years, and yes, I bragged about them to my friends. I have lain awake many nights wondering who was teaching you to drive, who was your first girlfriend, and how I would tease you about her, as if I were right there with you. I'm sorry for missing so much of you, Kent.

Love,
Daddy

As I stood looking at my special little boy, in a light gray coffin, I was dressed in bright orange coveralls. Prison guards were beside me. I wanted to reach out and touch him just once more, but the chains on my wrists wouldn't allow it.

It took a mortician to cover that cut on Kent's lip and get his hair to lay down. I'm so awfully sorry for missing the last eight years of Kent's life. If only I could have another chance to be the daddy he wanted me to be—the daddy he deserved. If I could just tickle Kent's back once more, or share some secret with him, or tease him and hold him for just a few minutes. God, I would gladly die for the chance.

Kent was killed when he was crushed under a tractor in an accident near Kelso, Washington. He is buried in Mt. Pleasant Cemetery, near the only tree there. So, if you are ever near that cemetery, and see a six-foot, five-inch, 270-pound beat-up old man on his knees beside that grave, praying to God in shame, you will know why.

Hopefully you will better understand why I wish he could have read this letter while he was alive. There are so many things I should have told him. So much time I should have spent with him.

If you have a special child in your life, please don't, for any reason, miss one single second with that child. Don't let what happened to me happen to you. Those moments are so awfully important.

To the lady officer with the special little sunray catcher— please believe me when I say, "For God's sake, spend every single precious moment with your child, now! This could be your last chance, because sometimes very special children don't get any older."

Ken "Duke" Monse'Broten

Light Came and Went and Came Again

When you make the finding yourself—even if you're the last person on Earth to see the light— you'll never forget it.

Carl Sagan

This title came from *Light in August* by William Faulkner and did, at one time, describe my life in jail. It was day then night then day again. It was simply a life of nonexistence, waiting to see how long they would keep me this time.

In my heart I'd once perceived a light that shone with love. Yet in jail that light seemed to fade as I centered on myself: shame, disgrace, anger, all those emotions that erupt when we perceive ourselves as "nonpersons." Life had no meaning. I wanted out.

Yes, to take the easy way out would hurt a few others, but they could overcome it and probably be better off in the long run. I'd reached the point where all my mental energy was directed toward devising a quick, easy and painless transition from this world to the next. I even felt a small twinge of joy at the prospect of being free from jail.

Yet on December 17, 1991, just one day before the forty-first anniversary of my own birth, God sent me an angel. I hadn't seen the angel's face yet, but I could feel a spark where the light once had been. Inside of me there was a growing new desire for life that I wanted to share.

Just two months after the birth of my granddaughter, the angel, my wife Connie and our daughter Missy came to visit. Missy held the angel in her arms. Her name was Chelsea Nicole. Soft, downlike hair made the crown of her head look dark brown. Brown eyes, and skin the color of fresh cream told me that this Angel was alive—she was real! She was doing what all of humanity does naturally in the presence of unconditional love. She was smiling—and she was looking at me, her Paw-Paw Willie!

Later in my cell I tried to put my feelings in writing. Our language didn't seem to have the words. I know well how my love for Connie made me ache inside for the privilege to hold her close. Even my love for my children made sense when I thought of always wanting to be on hand as their calm in the storm of life.

But what was this new love that made me ache to hold the little bundle in my arms, to caress those little cheeks, to sniff the down on her head? I felt a love building in me without bounds; a love that said I want to live, to love, to overcome whatever evil lurks in my heart, stealing my freedom again and again.

In the months that followed, my wife became what all parents claim they'll never be: a baby-sitter on twenty-four-hour, no-warning call. And neither Connie nor I would have had it any other way. Chelsea's presence seemed to work as a bonding agent, and a whole new relationship was being born.

Every Sunday morning I called home to talk to Connie, and I always said a prayer that Chelsea would be there too. At first Connie would hold the phone to Chelsea's ear so I could tell her how much I love her. As the months passed, she began to coo and laugh into the phone. It shocked me that so much time had passed when Chelsea said, "I love you, Paw-Paw."

On Thanksgiving Day 1997, twenty days before my angel Chelsea would be six years old, I dialed my wife's number. Chelsea was there!

With a heart full of love for a family I couldn't even see, I asked to speak to Chelsea. "Hello, Chelsea baby," I said.

"Hello, Paw-Paw Willie."

"I love you, Sweetie."

Chelsea didn't answer.

"Chelsea baby?"

"Paw-Paw Willie, why did you leave us and go to prison?"

My heart seemed to stop. Tears of shame flooded my eyes as I groped around in my mind for words. "I'm sorry" was all I could find.

"Paw-Paw Willie, will you come home soon?" she asked, and then added, "I love you a lot."

"I'll come as soon as I can, Sweetie."

Chelsea's question didn't come as a surprise. I knew I'd be in prison for the first nine years of her life. But in my limited intelligence, I expected one day she would ask something like: "Why did they put you in prison?" The wisdom of my angel's questions left no doubt who is responsible for this mess. Six-year-old Chelsea knows what we prison inmates seldom know at forty-six. No one took her Paw-Paw away. He left on his own.

The light came with my angel, went with the shame, and came again with the love of this angel.

Willie B. Raborn

"Louie here was framed, and I was set up."

Being a "Souper" Parent

Whether it's raising a child or running a corporation or molding the character of a cellmate, everyone has the opportunity to impact life.

Greg Barrett

Raising a child is never an easy task. Many times during the early years when I was raising my son alone, there simply was not enough money to pay the bills and buy nourishing food for a growing boy. So many of the evenings our meal consisted of what I called "combination soup." If we had corn, beans or other vegetables left from previous meals, we couldn't afford to waste anything. We were the original Tupperware family, and whatever was left over in the refrigerator would magically evolve into what we called our "souper dinner." We managed to live healthily on our meager income, and dinner was always *interesting*.

We amused ourselves by recalling which evening we had the black-eyed peas or what our "corny" conversation had covered during the "corny" dinner. Once my son, Paul, said to me, "You probably know more than a hundred ways to make soup, don't you?" My delightful little redheaded son would often tease me because I enjoyed eating soup so much. In later years, when times were better, often I'd prefer soup to a large dinner. He'd say, "Mom, I'm going to get you a T-shirt that says 'SOUPER MOM.' Will you wear it?"

Of course I would have been proud to wear that shirt, but it was not to be. Paul was murdered in 1985 while he was away at college. He had offered a ride to a very troubled seventeen-year-old, who shot my son when Paul refused to give up his car.

When I had the courage to open the boxes that had been packed from Paul's college apartment and brought to my home, I was surprised to see that he had kept all of the birthday cards I had given him since he was a child. Even though he had been away at a college only two hundred miles from home, he had kept all of the letters that I had ever mailed to him. Even more interesting were the notes he had saved through the years. Notes I had left on his door, notes left on the fridge when I had to work late, notes when he came in from school, instructions on chores he must do, what was left for him to snack on, or just little notes thanking him for things he remembered to do for me. Though the notes were not intended to be keepsakes, they were all filled with my love for Paul.

When Paul was in elementary school, he accompanied my parents on a ten-day trip from Texas to California. I knew their travel schedule, so well in advance I prepared a series of letters to Paul. We had never been apart for that long before, and I wanted him to know that even though he was away on an adventure, I still thought of him every day. In advance of the trip, I mailed letters to Paul at the motels along their route where they would be spending the night. On each letter addressed to "Mr. Paul Hines," I had written "Hold for Guest Arrival" above his name.

I can only imagine the delight he must have felt as he was handed his letter each night when they checked into their motel. He called me every night, and I could hear the joy and excitement in his voice. He felt so very important! In some of the letters I pasted cutouts from magazines, inserted my less-than-artistic drawings and created "picture-letters" for him to read.

Other letters contained bits of history about what they would see the next day and estimated the time that he should be on the lookout for a particular historical location. He not only received my love but also a bit of history. I'm not sure if he kept every note that I ever wrote to him. What's so precious to me now is that there are so many notes that he kept.

Parents are absent from their children's lives for many reasons. Being away from our children doesn't mean we stop being the parent they want and need so desperately. The statistics are startling: Seventy percent of inmates who are incarcerated in the state of Texas, where I live, were raised without a father or father figure in their home.

For over five years, I have volunteered to speak in prisons and give inspirational and motivational talks to inmates. As I relate my painful childhood, inmates nod in understanding; we share many common bonds. Many letters I receive from them contain descriptions of the loneliness they felt during their early years due to the absence of one or both of their parents. They also express their pain of not being able to be a proper parent. My presentations include parenting skills and the importance of continuing to be a parent regardless of distance. I also leave inmates information on how to receive free literature on becoming a better parent.

Thirteen years after Paul's murder, I arranged to meet and talk face-to-face with his murderer. It was a very powerful and life-changing experience for both of us. We talked for eight hours. At the end of our time together, I asked my Great Creator to give me what I needed to reach my hand to him across that table. Yes, I was able to do that. When I reached out, my hand held the hand that thirteen years earlier had held the pistol, and I touched the finger that pulled the trigger to murder my son.

There was a great release of anguish as I took that step. By reaching out, our joined hands created a bridge for my son's murderer to walk across and change his life, if he wanted to. The transition he has made since is miraculous. My son's murderer had 148 disciplinary cases in thirteen years. In the eleven months following our meeting, he had only two. Since our meeting, every month I write him an encouraging letter or send him a card.

As parents we must be very creative in raising our children. Teens and young adults in our society are desperately searching for love.

Thomas Ann Hines

A Convict's Letter to His Son

By the time we're old enough to stop being ashamed of our father, we have children who are old enough to be ashamed of us.

Larry King

Dear Son,

This is the hardest letter I have ever had to write. But I want you to hear the truth.

I am in prison because I broke the law. Your mother is not to blame for my being here. And you are not to blame for my being here. It is entirely my own fault. I broke the law, and now I must pay a penalty.

Because I am away from you both does not mean that I do not love you. There is nothing you could have done to change what has happened to me.

Listen to your mother. You might think that she is being too hard on you when she tells you what to do. The reason we have rules is so you will know that some things you do can get you into trouble with other people.

Rules are just like laws. They help us all keep peace in our family and in our neighborhood. Rules and laws are good for everyone, not just for you. It would be a very bad world if everyone decided for themselves which rules or laws they wanted to obey.

Just because you don't like a law is no reason to break it. Some laws may seem unfair but until they are changed, you will have no choice but to obey them. Otherwise, when you get older you could end up like me . . . in prison.

It would break my heart if you ever ended up like me, in a place like this. Prison is an ugly place. I do not have the freedom to be with you and Mom. I cannot go to McDonalds for a hamburger with you whenever I want. I cannot take you fishing as I used to. Prison guards watch me every moment of the day and decide when I will eat . . . when I will sleep . . . when I will do everything that I take for granted in the free world. There are some very mean people in here, and there are some very fine people in here. I try to associate with the ones who are not violent and destructive.

It is hard being a man and facing the truth. But when you make a mistake, you are the only one who can correct it. It is up to you to do everything that you can to undo any harm or pain you may have caused.

When I talk with you like this it is because I love you, and I want to help you avoid the mistakes I have made.

A real man does not blame others for his own behavior. A real man does not think that everything in life is free. He understands that there is always a price to pay for every action. When you break a rule or a law, you not only hurt others but you hurt yourself. Don't blame your mother or me when you make a mistake. Be a man and learn from your own mistakes.

Someday I will return home to you and your mother. Until then I want you to know that I think of you both a lot, and I love you both very much.

Obey your mother. Respect her and love her because

she needs you now more than ever. Because I failed is no
reason for you to fail. Let my mistake be a way for you to
learn as I have learned.

You have a good life ahead of you. Don't waste any part
of it as I have done.

Love,
Dad

Lou Torok

Beautiful Music

Music attracts the angels in the universe.

Bob Dylan

Paulette, a divorced mother of two, began volunteering at a state prison in 1992 by helping organize a speaking group for the inmates. After a few months, she was asked by the prison chaplain if she would consider joining the prison choir—The Heavenly Voices. Loving to sing, or as she puts it, "making a joyful noise," she jumped at the chance to join the all-inmate, all-male choir. It wasn't long before Paulette became an integral part of the choir members' lives as well—writing letters for them, contacting family members on their behalf, or just listening when they needed to talk.

One of the inmates she grew close to was Reggie. In 1990, Reggie had received a twenty-year sentence for drug trafficking. Because of his incredible voice and ability to command respect, he soon became the director of the prison choir. The choir rehearsed every day, and the members had to be particularly dedicated in order to belong. In addition to concerts and programs, they sometimes put on plays or had special anniversary parties for some of the members. The choir became a family of sorts within the confines of the prison walls.

In 1997, Reggie had his sentence reduced and was ordered to attend a drug and alcohol treatment program that assisted inmates in their transition back to society. Reggie was instructed to find someone to be his "host" during the program. He wrote letters to three people he thought would accept the responsibility, but he only received one reply—from Paulette.

During their years in the choir together, Paulette had grown to respect Reggie and she didn't feel that she could refuse his request. After passing inspection by the state as an appropriate host, Paulette was cleared to assist Reggie in his journey back into society. At first, restricted by the few free hours he had a week, Paulette's responsibilities were merely to act as Reggie's taxi driver to choir rehearsals, as The Heavenly Voices also had an "outside" choir made up of several ex-inmates and their wives. Soon, however, Reggie had more and more free hours as the intensive transition counseling began to lessen. Paulette often included him in family events. She heard from more than one relative and friend that she and Reggie made a "perfect" couple.

Her first reaction was to laugh off these comments, but she soon found herself more and more anxiously awaiting Reggie's weekend visits. She told herself it was because he was such a dear friend, one whose company she cherished. It wasn't until the day that Reggie was to be released from the program that she realized the true extent of her feelings.

She and her teenage son arrived at the halfway house at 5:45 A.M. to pick up Reggie and his belongings and to take him to live in the basement apartment of her home.

Instead, she was told that Reggie still had something on his record in his home state. Reggie was taken back to prison for possible extradition. Paulette, usually calm and in control, began to cry. She got in her car and raced home to begin a series of phone calls to find someone to help Reggie with this new legal entanglement. Ultimately, Reggie was delayed for only another week before being released into Paulette's custody. She realized then that she could no longer hide her feelings for him.

Although it had taken her more than five years, Paulette had finally realized that she had slowly but surely fallen in love with Reggie. If he hadn't known her feelings before, Reggie certainly knew when Paulette kissed him the day he was released. Paulette braced herself for the negative comments she was sure would come her way, but not one family member or friend said anything negative. It seemed Reggie had won the hearts of everyone in Paulette's life, including her son's and daughter's.

Reggie and Paulette were married on Valentine's Day 1999 and are still making beautiful music together with The Heavenly Voices. Some would argue that the chain of events that brought Reggie and Paulette together was just coincidence or fate, but Paulette firmly believes God planned it from the start. How else would Reggie have had a long prison sentence miraculously shortened?

Reggie is now serving a life sentence with the woman who is, above all else, his best friend.

Kimberly Raymer

Mom's Final Act

*Success is never final and failure is never fatal.
It's courage that counts.*

Jules Ellinger

Being in prison, a person has plenty of time to think, and for me the past thirteen years have been filled with memories of the past. In the lonely hours of night, my mind sweeps back to the most significant events of my life, and oh so often, back to Mom, and her final act.

Her eyes were dark and sad, and her face seemed to reflect many more years than she had actually lived. She was a handsome woman at best but in my eyes, she was beautiful.

Mom lived a hard life but always took time to show us six children that we were loved. She prided herself on always being there with the answer to our every need, and someone always needed something. Clearly I recall the sounds of home. "Mom, my shirt needs ironing. Mom, I need help with my homework. Mom, what's for dinner? Mom, I need this, and Mom, I need that." Mom was always the answer—no one gave it a second thought. I suppose our whole family just figured, this is what she lived for.

There were three meals a day, not one ever late; six children—all in school, complete with packed lunches, and always wearing clean clothes, even though they were sometimes patched.

Our old two-story house was far from fancy, but was always clean from top to bottom. There was no inside plumbing, but somehow Mom always managed to have plenty of hot water for baths and cleaning. Our clothes were always washed and ironed. We never questioned the hot roaring fire we woke up to on cold winter mornings, or the hot breakfast awaiting us on the table. We never questioned anything that Mom did for us each day, so unselfishly and without complaining. We selfishly took it all for granted.

I suppose everyone has regrets in life. I'll always regret taking Mom for granted, and I'll never forget the last opportunity I had to right this wrong. Mom's final act, of fulfilling one last need, will be with me forever.

I was sixteen and working my first real job at a gas station. Just as she had with my dad and my older brothers, Mom would wake me bright and early for work and breakfast would be waiting on the table. This became a ritual I accepted as a way of life—that is, until one spring morning in 1966.

As usual, Mom woke me for work, but something in the tone of her voice was different. I entered the kitchen, eager for breakfast. For the first time since I could remember, the table was empty. I was totally confused, but she simply told me I'd have to fix a bowl of cereal myself because she didn't feel well. I steamed as I thought, *How could she NOT have my breakfast ready?* For the first time in my life, I yelled at my mom, left the house and slammed the door behind me.

As the morning passed, I began feeling really bad about the way I acted. I was looking forward to the end of the day when I could go home, apologize and make things right between us. About 11 A.M. the phone rang and the voice on the other end said simply, "You need to come home right away, Roger. Your mom's dead."

It was a shocking discovery—a self-inflicted bullet wound through the heart had taken her life. No suicide note, no warnings, no answers. In my mind, there could have been only one reason—me.

Days and weeks passed, and the guilt of a sixteen-year-old boy grew unbearable. I had to talk to my mom.

At the cemetery I stood alone at her graveside and cried. I tried to tell her how sorry I was, and that I needed her to forgive me, but in my heart, I knew it was too late. As I arrived home that day, my sister ran out to meet me. Holding a piece of paper in her hand, she said, "I found this in Mom's Bible today. It's addressed to you." My hands trembled, and tears stung my eyes as I read:

Dear Roger,

I love you. I know, after the way we left things this morning, you'll need to hear from me this one last time. Outside of God Himself, I probably know you better than anyone. I think I have an idea of how you must be feeling about now, but Son, please don't feel guilty. What I'm about to do is no one's fault, least of all yours. There really is no answer, so don't waste your life trying to find one. With all my children grown now, I feel it's time for me to rest.

I know you're feeling guilty, Son, but it is I who prays for your forgiveness. I hope you know I do forgive you for getting angry, and I love you so very much.

I've always tried to take care of all your needs, Son, and I pray that this little note will take care of what I'm sure you're needing most right now.

I Love You,
Mom

In what must have been the most confusing moments of her life, my mom's final act of love and forgiveness fulfilled my greatest need.

Now I stare out across a dark and empty prison yard, and realize how dark and empty my own life has been without her. If only she had told me how she felt. If only I had listened. I guess she could not have known how much I would always need her.

Within these walls, this prison,
My mind and thoughts run free.
I think of Mom and days gone by,
And of what she meant to me.

I wonder how life would have been
Had she not gone away,
And would I be behind these bars,
If she were here today?

How would my life be different?
I've asked a million times,
If I could only talk to her,
She might have stopped my crimes.

I'm thankful for the time we had,
But she could not have known
Of the dark void left within my life
In the years since she's been gone.

I needed her and miss her.
I love her—for a fact,
But I know my life is different,
Because of Mom's final act.

R. L. Todd

The Promised Visit

There is so much about prison life that can never be captured with words. This utter loneliness should never be forced on anyone that once knew freedom.

Kenneth Hodge

After hearing about men who while in prison lost a loved one, I'd think to myself, *How sad. That's life.* I've seen fellow inmates as they received word of a loved one's death and I think, *Take time to grieve, but move on.*

One day, I was called into the chaplain's office. He said, "Your mom died."

Time stood still. Everything froze. I quickly went into an instant replay of my last conversation with Mom. I thought of the warmth in her voice, the words of love and my promise that I'd be home soon.

I thought of how much love she spread everywhere she went. The world wouldn't be quite the same. I wanted to cry but couldn't. If I cried, it would mean that Mom was dead. No. I promised her I'd be home to visit her, to enjoy a home-cooked meal, to tell her how I spent my time in here and assure her I was okay.

I wanted to witness to her how prayers touched my life. This wasn't something that would ever happen to me. Only other men in prison lost a loved one.

When I phoned home, we all cried. I heard them say, "Stay strong. Mom loves you and is in heaven now. Life goes on. We'll be there to see you soon. We'll arrange for you to have a viewing at the funeral home."

I went to the viewing for an hour and cried the entire time. I didn't stop crying even though I was under the watchful eyes of the guards and an occasional passing of funeral home employees. I cried and prayed over her body. I kept my promise of coming home the best I could. I was with her and out of prison for an hour. She was pleased. She was at peace and so was I. In prayer, I still talk to her, and life goes on.

Ron Ambrosia

Unsung "Sheroes"

*Trust men and they will be true to you; treat
them greatly and they will show themselves great.*

Ralph Waldo Emerson

Unfortunately, the wives and family members left
behind are the second victims of the crimes committed by
inmates. Many of the women become the unsung
"sheroes" doing as the country song says, "Stand by your
man." These women are a blessing to their inmate men as
they serve their time.

It is not unusual for women to drive to prisons hundreds of miles away in desolate places, just to spend a few
hours with their loved ones. During my years as a prison
chaplain, I watched faithful wives, family members and
fiancées make tremendous sacrifices in order to be supportive of their loved ones behind bars. Many times the
families pay a greater price for the crime than the incarcerated. The hands-on decisions and responsibilities are
transferred from the inmate to the ones they leave behind.
The inmates' sole responsibility is to abide by regulated
routines of waking, eating, working, playing and sleeping.

One "shero," middle-aged Mrs. Helen Thomas, faithfully visited her husband Bill monthly and every holiday during the eight years he served for embezzlement. She had been a privileged homemaker whose life revolved around her family and the community. Suddenly everything changed when Bill was arrested, tried, convicted and incarcerated. Their lives and their children's lives were turned upside down. The once-proud family went through agony and embarrassment. Their life savings suffered a major blow as Mrs. Thomas used it and a second mortgage to pay the legal fees.

"Things are so different now," she told me. "Chaplain, before Bill's arrest, I never had to do anything but take care of my home. Now all the responsibility is mine. My driving was limited to getting around town to shop in the mall and the grocery store—no more! In order to see Bill, I have to drive ten hours one way for our weekend visit. Thank God my children, who are suffering themselves, are so supportive. My son found me a job, and he keeps my car running."

Many times she left the institution in bad weather or was simply too tired to make it home that night. She endured the extra expense of staying in a motel until the next morning to continue her journey. Bill was always anxious when she left the institution alone, and I placed calls for him to find out if she arrived safely when the weather was bad. Despite the sacrifice, she never missed a monthly visit during his incarceration. I am happy to say that six years after Bill's release, we're still in contact. Bill is an appreciative man who has resumed his responsibilities, and his family is doing beautifully. He joyfully admits that his "shero" is what made the difference.

There are many heroes and sheroes like Helen Thomas waiting for their mates to come home. They are called upon to accomplish unfamiliar tasks. Through God's grace and their faith, they find the strength, courage and ability to meet the challenges. I salute and respect these faithful, committed mates.

To the inmates fortunate enough to have one of these "sheroes," I say cherish her. I remind the inmates of God's words in Proverbs 31: "When one finds a worthy wife, her value is far beyond pearls. Her husband, entrusting his heart to her, has an unfailing prize. She brings him good, and not evil, all the days of her life. Strength and honor are her clothing."

George Castillo

Putting on the Mask

Pain is synonymous with spirituality. When you're in the most pain, you're closest to God.

Derrick Johnson

Every year I go through the same routine. After nine years one would think it becomes easier, but instead it hurts more and more. It is harder each year to pretend, to put on the mask, when my heart feels so empty. The presents are being wrapped and families gather together to rejoice the holidays. Why can't I? Why must my holidays be full of such loneliness? I didn't do anything wrong. All I ever wanted for my children was to know they were loved and to be truly happy with themselves. I did the best I knew how to raise my children. I'm sure I made mistakes, but I always did my best. Love can be a double-edged sword. Maybe I loved too much.

Deep inside my tears are building. At night, all alone, the dam breaks and the tears pour out. Alone in the dark, I beg God that my daughter, Cary, is all right and to bring her home to me, alive. I wonder when enough really is enough. How much more can I endure? Why does it seem so easy for people, especially family, to forget? Forget the one who isn't there? One would think that family would truly understand the void you are feeling. One would think that family would want to talk about all the children during the holidays, but one would be wrong. My family says they don't mention her name because they don't want to upset me. But it hurts worse with the silence. Cary is a part of me. She is a part of my world. How can I keep putting on the mask? Why do I have to?

Prison brings pain to everyone. Each time I walk through the prison gates, I pray Cary is all right. Each time I walk out of the gates, the tears fall like a river. I hurt for my child. Through the years of her incarceration I've watched the petals of my beautiful rose become torn and scarred. Like the thorns on a rose, Cary caused herself pain trying to survive in the world known as prison. Only those who live behind those cold walls of prison know the reality it takes to survive. I pray that she still believes in herself, just as I still believe in her.

The walls of prison are cold and uncaring. Cary comes to me with her own mask on. She tries to pretend, for a short while, that everything is "normal." Her mask tries to hide her pain and disappointments. She watches my face and searches for and finds the hope. She knows the one thing that will never disappear is my love for her. She is part of who I am. She makes me who I am—her mother.

Cary cries when I leave. She becomes so angry with herself for the pain her wrong choices have caused so many people. She cries not only for her pain, but for mine. Prison is not a place to show tears, not even during our visits, because there is always someone who will take advantage of those tears. In prison tears are a sign of weakness, so we must wear our masks, together. A hug, a smile, and we attempt to travel back in time—a time when prison was not a part of our lives. We look to the future—the future of life without prison. We talk about life outside of prison. We talk about the "what ifs" and the "could have beens."

As I leave the prison, waiting for the gates to open and close behind me, it feels like my heart is being ripped out. I'm leaving part of me behind. It's part of me that I can't hold or help. I can't be there when she cries. I hate prisons. I hate them with all my being. I watch what prison has done to my daughter's life and to mine. I have no control, no power to help my child. Helplessness to a mother is something unimaginable. I bore this child and I raised this child. I love this child and yet, in all her pain, I can't hold her. I can't make her pain go away, and it's killing me inside. I dream of the day I can visit my daughter in her own home and not have to be searched and talked down to by some correctional officer. I dream of a day when others don't hold this power over my life. I dream of a time when our meetings will bring joy, and we can put the cold prison walls behind us.

As the tears roll down my face, I can feel my daughter's pain. The emptiness inside me wants to scream out, but no one will hear. The mask covers the pain and only silence is heard until at night, when I'm all alone, the river of tears flows and won't stop. When I wake up, I carefully put the mask on, and begin again.

Linda Reeves
Submitted by Thomas Ann Hines

Where There's Faith

What is the price of experience?
Do men buy it for a song?
Or wisdom for a dance in the street?
No, it is bought with the price of all the man hath,
His house, his wife, his children.

William Blake

The hobby shop is a place where guys do woodwork, leather crafts, make jewelry and paint. Most are involved as a means to take their minds away from the length of their sentences, and to maintain an income above the four cents per hour that their prison jobs pay them. They sell their wares to security officers and other prison employees, and most make a decent profit, by prison standards.

Some inmates, however, have taken their trade to a different level. One such inmate is a man I will call Hobby Shop Joe. He entered Angola some time during the early 1970s for murder. He killed a guy who had approached his wife in a foul manner. The court didn't sympathize with his situation, and he found himself in the midst of a violent environment. Once here, his focus was directed toward two things. First, surviving in prison. Second, the survival of his wife and two children. His immediate solution to both problems was to pray. Like many inmates, he prayed a lot.

Prison existence is hard on families. Rarely do they survive lengthy terms of confinement. Sometimes, due to bitter breakups, children are reared never knowing their father's love, and at times, not knowing who their fathers are. Hobby Shop Joe was determined that his family was not going to fall into that category.

He kind of stayed to himself and didn't allow his lifestyle to offend or invade the territorial boundaries of others. Eventually, he met a guy who spent most of his nonworking hours in the hobby shop developing leather products: belts, purses, wallets, Bible covers. They became close associates and the guy allowed Joe to work as his helper. Joe caught on fast and soon found himself selling his products and making money. Every extra penny was sent to his wife and children. As time passed, Joe managed to obtain his own hobby shop box. He purchased leather and tools, and Joe developed a clientele. Each visiting day his wife and daughters were seen hauling off boxloads of belts, purses and other items. His wife found a gift shop that would sell his products, and when the owner of the shop found out that the money was to be used to help support Joe's family, the shop owner didn't charge Joe's wife a percentage fee.

That was over twenty years ago. Joe is still serving a life sentence, but his determination to keep his family together has seen his daughters grow up and go to college. Their tuition was paid with money made from his leather goods. Joe's wife has remained at his side.

It just goes to show you that, regardless of the situation, where there's faith there can be victory.

G. Ashanti Witherspoon
Submitted by Fran and Nigel Risner

Mail Call

Darkness and loneliness fill my cell
With pain and fear too great to yell.

I wait for the mailman to deliver to me
As I wipe away tears that no one will see.

I pray so sincere with head raised above,
"Please, God, soon send a letter of love."

I long to gaze upon pages so dear,
With riches to bring my loved ones near.

Words of diamonds on pages of gold
A message from heaven as their story is told,

"We love you, miss you, pray you'll be free."
A treasure-filled envelope just for me.

Please bring memories of joys I once knew
Family, friends and things I would do.

The darkness and pain of my cell will prevail
As my name, again, was not called for mail.

John M. Reynolds

Envy

*M*an *will do many things to get himself loved;
he will do all things to get himself envied.

Mark Twain

To the man, tired to the bone and having less than ten dollars in his pocket, coming home from work to a house that needs paint, a yard that needs mowing and is full of kids' toys and screaming children . . .

To the man who drives an old pickup that can't last much longer—one he still owes several payments on—who comes home to a wife dressed in old blue jeans, who's a little overweight, in a bad mood, wearing no makeup, and having uncombed hair and bad breath . . .

To the man whose dinner will consist of chicken noodle soup and hot dogs; from the prison cell from which I'm writing this, I say, "God, how I envy you!"

Ken "Duke" Monse'Broten

Just a Touch

I learned that it is the weak who are cruel, and that gentleness is to be expected only from the strong.

Leo Rosten

I just finished reading a book about some Catholic nuns working in Calcutta with dying leprosy patients. These caring and dedicated Sisters found they could comfort dying patients just by touching them. The touch—the gentle, loving touch from someone who cares—I know its importance.

I recall coming home after driving log-trucks all day, tired to the bone. It gets you right between the shoulders. After taking a nice hot shower, I would lay down right in the center of the living room, in the middle of the floor. I'd lie flat on my back, arms spread wide. I would just lie there. My sons were little then—in preschool. When they noticed me lying there, they stopped whatever they were doing. No healthy kid will pass up a chance to attack a grown person when he is flat on his back. I was in their world then; they could even look down at me for a change;

I was their size. If they were a bit slow to react, I just raised my head up, looked directly at them and stuck out my tongue. That would do it, I promise you. Not only was I in their world, I was mouthing off too. They would attack! I would hear tinkling giggles, squeals and even some grunts as they got me. I would enjoy the tinkle in their voices, see the sparkle in their eyes, join their laughter and be prepared for one hell of a battle. I would also notice the tension leave my body. Memories of a bad day at work, even the tension between my shoulders would be forgotten. I would grunt, laugh and suffer the beating they gave me. After ten or fifteen minutes of that, huffing and puffing, I sometimes said, "I give," to get out of some yet unnamed foolproof headlock that little boys know. Once they had won or lost—makes no difference—it was time to talk. Of course, I became something akin to a log at that point. They'd either sit on me or sit beside me and kinda lean on me.

"Ya know what, Dad? Billy found a green snake and he gots it in a jar."

"Hey, Dad, can you fix the wagon 'cause the wheel fell off?"

"Dad, if we had a thousand-million-hundred dollars, would it cover up the whole house an' everything?"

The trick was to really listen—to really hear them. I would notice what took place in me because of the touch of those little hands, their simple little world and the questions that honestly needed answers. I lived in their world for just a few minutes and looked up at those little faces as they asked questions of the smartest man they knew—Dad. They make the world simple, soft, close and completely honest.

You may even be lucky enough to share a secret or two. The bottom line is you have just been disarmed of the anger and tension you brought home.

I wonder if that touch—and that simple, honest, no-bullheaded world—isn't needed much more than people realize these days. I've laid in this prison cell so angry that my guts feel like they're vibrating, over something that's not even worth mentioning. I'm angry and surrounded by everything hard and cold, concrete and steel. We have programs here in prison called "Anger Management." I've taken them all and even facilitated a few. They tell you all kinds of tricks: count to ten, beat on a pillow, even hug a damn tree (that last one is called "getting grounded"). They have told me of yin and yang in relation to the psyche, of inside response to outside stimuli, and even of subconscious responses. With the exception of Gordon Graham's Breaking Barriers and A Framework for Recovery—programs designed by someone who has been there—it's a complicated line of pure speculation designed only to keep the designer out of the unemployment line or nuthouse.

What calms me is the love and the unguarded understanding of my children; the tinkle in their voices, their touch, their laughter and the honest closeness of them; and the gentle, caring touch of a woman who smells of laundry soap or dish soap—not Chanel No. 5. That's what calms an angry man. My anger these days is mostly at myself for being the damn fool that I am, as opposed to the man I could have been.

That anger, combined with guilt, comes to the surface because of a little boy with soft hands. Hands I've held so many times, yet not enough. I'm haunted by memories of that child being made to sit in the corner as punishment for some unremembered misdeed. That little boy, sitting facing the corner, sad and ashamed, because his dad was upset with him, alone and in silence.

I never could spank a child; can't stand to be around when one is spanked either. It's something about the fear in a child's eyes; possibly some hidden memory of the beatings I experienced as a little boy. Whatever the reason, I can't spank a child. So, when my sons messed up, I would make them sit in the corner for a while.

My son Kent was killed when he was fifteen years old, after being crushed under a farm tractor.

Do you have any idea of what I would give to be able to reclaim those lost minutes when I made Kent sit in that corner? I wonder how many tears I've shed as I prayed for one more chance to again wrestle with my little boys in the center of that living room floor. I would love to share their simple world, hear the joy in their laughter, feel the touch of their little hands and be called Daddy, just a couple more times.

I know nothing about leprosy or what those Catholic nuns must have experienced in Calcutta, but after countless nights alone in a prison cell, I do know what I miss the most and what calms me. A touch . . . just a gentle, loving touch from someone who cares.

Ken "Duke" Monse'Broten

A Father's Prayer

The ardent longing in my life
Is not a prayer for me;
In the deep watches of the night
I pray, not selfishly.
I lift six lives to You, O God,
Six hearts I know You love.
I cannot help them now below,
Please bless them from above.

You see their need as I cannot,
You hear their prayers, I know.
You feel their tears upon Your cheek,
Please hold them as I go.
No man could love them as I do,
No heart could miss them so.
But only You can lift their heads
And hold them as I go.

Give them strength when they are weak,
And peace in place of fear.
Give them eyes of faith that watch
As miracles appear.

Hold them close in Your embrace,
The way I know I would.
Hold them tight in Your embrace,
The way a father should.
Be their fortress from the storms,
A place where they can hide.
A father strong whom they can trust,
In You they can have pride.

Although I cannot touch a face,
Or hold my loved ones near,
Or see them in the morning light,
Or wipe away their tears,
Or talk with them about their day,
Or pray with them at night,
I know that You will be with them,
You'll be their guiding light.

I give them to You, one by one,
My wife and five dear stars.
Please keep them close and love them strong!
I'll love them from afar.

John W. Gillette Jr.

CLOSE TO HOME   JOHN McPHERSON

"Having encouraged homeowners to leave
a copy of *Chicken Soup for the Burglar's Soul*
on their coffee tables, police are able to
nail yet another loafing thief."

Reprinted by permission of John McPherson. Submitted by Robin A. Worman, Lieutenant Commander, US Navy, Retired.

$\overline{2}$

ON CHANGE

*I*ve never met a person, I don't care what
his condition, in whom I could not see
possibilities.
I don't care how much a man may consider
himself a failure,
I believe in him, for he can change the thing
that is wrong in his life anytime he is ready
and prepared to do it.
Whenever he develops the desire, he can take
away from his life the thing that is defeating it.
The capacity for reformation and change lies
within.

Preston Bradley

Reprinted by permission of Charles Carkhuff.

Bringing the Outside to the Inside

Each year every prison in our state conducts a full-scale exercise to practice our response to a serious security incident. As warden, I serve as the incident commander. It is always the most stressful day of the year for me.

At the end of one of these days, I was relieved that the scenario was over and was packing my briefcase to leave for ten days. I noticed a small piece of paper lying on my desk, and an inmate's name caught my eye. Only yesterday Tom, a Kairos volunteer, had asked me to see an inmate named David. He had just received news of his nephew's death—a suicide. I kept looking at that paper and could not bring myself to leave until I met with him.

I sent for David and we talked about his nephew Tim's death. It devastated him and his entire family. David had attended a Kairos spiritual retreat weekend, during which he developed a closer relationship with God. He said that he wished that his sister could experience a weekend like he had. The only problem is that this retreat is for men in prison.

I left for England three days later and traveled with a

woman named Jo Chapman. Several years ago, she founded a related ministry called Kairos Outside. It provides spiritual renewal weekends for women whose lives have been impacted by incarceration. Generally mothers, sisters, daughters and spouses attend. In the United States, the weekend is conducted at a church or retreat center. When I told Jo about David's story, I asked her if it would be possible to conduct the weekend inside the prison. That way, the inmates who sponsored their loved ones could also participate. Jo loved the idea and gave us the go-ahead.

A team of committed volunteers worked hard to prepare. Many details needed to be worked out, such as hotel arrangements for the "guests," logistics of holding the retreat in the prison chapel, security concerns, preparing the team and meal preparations.

The inmates also worked very hard. They wrote the theme song, "Right from the Heart," planted a garden, set up the chapel and worked behind the scenes preparing meals, writing letters and praying.

The first Kairos Outside held on the inside took place September 17 to 19, 1999, one year after the tragedy in David's family. His sister, along with thirty-five other women guests, participated in a weekend that none of us who attended would ever forget.

I have worked in corrections for over eighteen years and have been a prison warden for eleven of those. Kairos Outside, brought to the inside, was the most powerful event I have ever witnessed in a prison.

Christine Money

My Best Friend Jack

A true friend is someone who is there for you when he'd rather be anywhere else.

Len Wein

If there was anyone less likely to become my mentor, it was Smiling Jack. He was an ex-con who had left decades of drunken turmoil in his wake. Yet, by the time we met, Smiling Jack had transformed his life.

Raised in the mountains of North Carolina, there was little evidence that anything but a difficult future lay in Jack's path. His formal education ended in the third grade. His father and most of his relatives worked in the local sawmill, and it was assumed he would do the same. The only other option was working with the moonshiners. By the time he was a young teen, Jack had discovered the easy money of "running" corn liquor. Unfortunately, he also developed a taste for the bottled lightning and became his own best customer.

One fall evening, in a car filled with corn squeezings, unable to escape the pursuing revenuers, he was arrested. Sentenced to prison, he spent several years shackled at the ankles, working on a chain gang. Not surprisingly, the days and months of humiliation served only to increase his anger and bitterness at the world.

On his release, determined to escape the boredom of his hometown, he joined the merchant marines. Working aboard cargo ships, he traveled the world. Yet, lost in a haze of whiskey, each port was much the same as the one he'd just left—barrooms and trouble. Eventually the alcohol abuse took its toll and, no longer fit to work, he returned to the familiar mountains of North Carolina. He worked when and where he could, but only long enough to buy another jug of the clear liquid that controlled his life.

A passing carnival hired him as a maintenance mechanic, and so began a drunken tour of small-town America.

Weeks, months and years passed in a blur. Increasingly, he awoke in jail cells with cuts and bruises that he couldn't explain. Eventually fired from the carnival, he found himself in an unfamiliar, small town in Pennsylvania. Odd jobs kept him in liquor for a time. As his health deteriorated, he became incapable of even the simplest labor.

In the last, deadly stages of alcoholism he collected welfare and had whiskey delivered to his shabby, rented room. When his check was late, drinking after-shave became a reasonable alternative. One evening Jack was found unconscious in an alcohol-induced coma and was rushed to the emergency room.

While in the hospital, doctors convinced him to seek treatment. Having nowhere else to turn, he accepted. That became the turning point in his life. By the time I met Jack, it had been several years since he had "taken" any liquor.

I had screwed up a good career in New York City. In the process, I'd alienated everyone I knew. Overwhelmed by self-pity and depression, for several years I hid in the bottom of a gin bottle, afraid to live but even more terrified to die. For reasons I still don't understand,

Providence stepped in and, after receiving much-needed help, I started the difficult task of putting my life back together. I moved to a small town to start over. And more than a year later, my career prospects were improving steadily. But emotionally, I was not doing well. That's when I first met Jack.

While I was staring at a lobby office directory for several minutes, a little, round man in blue work clothes waddled toward me. Grinning at my confusion, he pointed me in the right direction.

I hadn't taken more than a few steps when, in a friendly Southern drawl, he called after me, "And by the way, Son, I don't recall when I've last seen a feller look as down in the mouth as you."

Surprised at this personal observation, I turned toward him. With an almost sad, yet sincere expression, this stranger looked me in the eye and said softly, "Son, if nobody's told you they loved you today—I do." With keys jingling, he turned and disappeared through a door into the stairwell.

This warm, smiling janitor touched my heart. I'd find excuses to visit "his" office building. Sitting in his cluttered, basement office we made small talk. Gradually I came to recognize the priceless experience and wisdom he was giving me. When we walked along Main Street, passing cars honked greetings and shop owners stepped out to say hello. I marveled at the magical effect this once-hopeless man had on people. "Every day is a blessing," he would tell me. "I shoulda been dead a long time ago, but for some reason the good Lord seen fit to give me a second chance—I aim to use it to help folks."

His philosophy for living was simple. "Live a day at a time and do the best you can. Ask the Good Lord to look after you when you wake up, and thank him before you go to sleep."

I saw him lend money to people, knowing he would probably not be repaid. If someone admired something he owned, more than likely he would make it their gift.

My career came together and I was working again on Madison Avenue. With Jack's support and friendship, my personal life turned around. I met and fell in love with a remarkable woman, and a year after we met, this beautiful lady agreed to become my wife.

On a breezy, summer afternoon I stood at the church altar wearing an ill-fitted tuxedo and a comfortable grin. Accompanied by organ music, the love of my life, radiant in her lace wedding gown, slowly made her way down the center aisle.

The priest posed the question, "Who gives this woman away?" For a fleeting moment, the altar glowed as if enveloped by a mist of pastels, and the clean, fresh scent of approaching rain drifted through the church. As I took my bride's hand, we looked into the misty, blue eyes of the one whose love and guidance had made this day possible. My best friend, Jack, smiled at us and proudly responded, "I do."

George M. Roth

Another Gold Nugget

*We have been taught to believe that negative
equals realistic and positive equals unrealistic.*

Susan Jeffers

I've been in prison twelve years, serving a sentence of
life without parole for robbing a bank in Mobile, Alabama.
Anxiety, fear, frustration and failed escape attempts—
coupled with numerous trips to the "hole"—filled the first
five of those years.

Six years ago it dawned on me. The reason my life was so
full of negativity, anger and despair was because I challenged
life. I met it with negativity, anger and despair. The simple
and overused phrase, "What goes around comes around," hit
home. I finally understood what was meant by that.

During my last trip to the hole, I thought, *Man, I'm so
tired of this. Every time I turn around I'm being hassled. Why does
this keep happening to me? I didn't do anything. I don't understand
why they locked me up.* The previous day, a correctional officer shook down my living area. While he was trying to do
his job, I cursed, kicked the foot of my bunk and became
belligerent.

A few nights later, I awakened suddenly and jumped out of bed. "What goes around comes around" kept playing over and over inside my head.

If that's true, I thought, *then I keep gettin' screwed up because of what I'm doing. If I'm having angry and frustrating experiences all the time, then it must be because I'm responding to the world in an angry and frustrating manner.*

Recalling a dream I had, I saw a clear image of a large wicker basket. I was placing baseball-sized rocks into this basket, one after another. When I stood on a ladder to look inside this tall basket, all I saw were rocks.

I thought, *If day after day I keep putting rocks into this basket, what can I expect to find when I reach inside?* The answer was simple—rocks! So it is with our lives.

Christian doctrine tells us that, we reap what we sow. Islamic doctrine states that not one of us is a believer until our love for our brother and ourselves, and Native American doctrine tells us that we should not condemn a brother until we have walked a mile in his moccasins.

These are fundamental truths. It has taken twelve years in prison and much pain to myself and others to reach the point where I finally recognize the validity of these truths. I've been a little slow at times!

Still, I had to ask myself, *Why should I be concerned about my brother? Why should I care about what I do to him? Why should I love for him what I would love for myself? Why should I seek to understand him?*

Because what I do to him, what I think of him, what I want for him, will either be the gold or the rock that I put into the basket of my life. What I do to you, I do to myself.

We often do terrible things, such as commit an unlawful act or treat someone cruelly, and later think we have gotten away with it, that we won't have to suffer the consequences of our actions. It may take fifty years for the effect to catch up with the cause, but be ready, it's coming!

Here's the good news: If we give respect and love, respect and love are what we get back. Six years ago, while sitting in the hole, I made another selfish decision. I was tired of negativity and bad experiences in my life. I wanted some of the good experiences that I saw other people having. Silently, I made a vow, *Today, just for twenty-four hours, I'm going to try an experiment, and I'm not going to tell anyone. I'm going to try hard to give respect, love and understanding to everyone I meet, in every situation, no matter how difficult. If it's true that what we give is what we get, then I want some.*

I kept doing this and kept having good days. That was six years ago, and I've had many good days since.

I still have a sentence of life without parole, and I'm still reaping the consequences of my long-term negative behavior, but that continues to improve. I'm putting together a string of good days to balance the bad days that comprise my life. When the rocks have all been replaced with gold nuggets, I'll reach into the basket and gold nuggets will be all I find.

R. Troy Bridges

So Can You!

Our task must be to free ourselves from this prison by widening our circles of compassion to embrace all living creatures and the whole of nature in its beauty.

Albert Einstein

Bill Sands had been a convict in San Quentin. When he left prison, he started writing, authored a book called *My Shadow Ran Fast* about his experiences as a convict and eventually became a public speaker. Mark Victor Hansen had the privilege of listening to him one night when he was in college. Bill was in front of an audience of about fifteen hundred students who, in their sophomoric innocence, thought they knew it all. Bill stood up there and said something like this: "My parents didn't like themselves. My father was a federal judge, my mother an alcoholic, and the only way I could get their attention was to do something like throwing a brick through a storefront window. Then I started robbing stores and got into more and more serious crimes and finally ended up in San Quentin.

"When I got there, they asked me to engage in perverted sexual activity. When I wouldn't, they broke my nose." At this point Bill pressed his nose flat to his face in front of those fifteen hundred students. "When they persisted and I resisted, they broke all the fingers in my hand." He bent all his fingers back ninety degrees.

Bill Sands had the attention of every one of those know-it-all students riveted on him. He continued with his story about feeling that he was the "losingest" person who had ever lived. Every one of us has shared that feeling or thought it at some time in his or her life. Bill felt that losing was such a natural state of things for him that he couldn't conceive of anything different.

Then the warden, Clinton Duffy, took an interest in him. This warden read the histories of all the prisoners and saw something special in Bill. He gave him a copy of Napoleon Hill's book *Think and Grow Rich,* and Bill read the principles and read the ideas between the lines.

Bill decided that he was going to succeed—succeed by helping other prisoners. He wrote down his goals and talked about his goals, and even dreamed about his goals.

Even though he was in prison for life, Bill eventually was paroled, and he immediately started the Seven Step Foundation, which helped ex-convicts make it on the outside. He wrote his book about being a convict and talked about it on national tours such as the one Mark had attended at Southern Illinois University's Convocation Series. Almost instantly he became wealthy and successful.

By the time he was nearly finished speaking that night, he had made those students stand up, sit down, laugh, cry and decide to change their lives. (He was one of the reasons Mark Victor Hansen eventually decided to go into public speaking.)

Finally, at the end of his talk, Bill said, "I want to introduce my wife, the most beautiful woman in my life." The curtain opened and she came out. Mark held his breath. With the arrogance of youth, he immediately decided that she was anything but beautiful. But the audience, women first, gave her a standing ovation. As one, they seemed to say that if a great man like Bill Sands could see beauty in her, then she must indeed be beautiful.

Bill Sands, the "losingest" man who ever lived, by his own admission—and certainly by the condemnation of others—had become a personality so powerful that he could touch people to the very fiber of their being. He had seen through and cast aside that great excuse about losing that had kept him back. He had replaced a negative mental attitude with a positive mental attitude (PMA—it also stands for Pays More Always). He had taken a problem and found within it the seeds of an opportunity. His life's calling was not to be a convict. It was to be an author, a speaker, a businessman and a counselor. He had broken through. So can you!

Jack Canfield and Mark Victor Hansen

A Lot of Bread

Drugs deceive! First drugs thrill—then drugs kill!

Leola Hoekstra
International Prison Ministry

When I was first incarcerated in 1987, the hardest part of doing prison time was being away from my children. This is common with most of the women in prison, so often stories of our children are shared among each other.

Renee, a friend I had met in prison, was doing seven years for drug charges. She had a five-year-old son that her parents were raising. She and the grandparents had told the five-year-old that Renee was away at school in order to protect him from the fear and humiliation of his mother being incarcerated. Renee would call her son often and promise him that it wouldn't be long before they'd be reunited again.

One evening, after talking to her son, Renee came to me with tears in her eyes. Her son had asked if she would be home soon. Renee made the regular promise that it wouldn't be too much longer now. The boy asked, "Can we go to the duck pond when you get home?" She assured him that they would.

In the innocence of a child, he had proudly announced that he was saving up the bread already. Renee's heart wrenched imagining the huge pile of moldy bread that would be piled up before she would be able to keep her promise to this trusting five-year-old.

We cried together, and she somehow made it through the crisis. I was shocked when only a few weeks later she came to me seeking advice. She had just received her state pay—twenty-five dollars for the month—and had the opportunity to buy a half of a pill for twenty-five dollars. It would leave her broke for the rest of the month, but Renee really wanted to buy the pill. It would be dissolved and shot up for a high. She felt that she deserved the "treat" because prison was so hard, she was so lonely and it was almost her birthday. I'm sure Renee had other reasons, but my head was still spinning from the fact that she could even consider it with a five-year-old son waiting to share her life with him.

Since I don't do drugs and never have, I couldn't imagine what kind of high could be greater than spending time with your child. Before I realized what I was saying, I blurted out, "You're grown, and you have to make your own decisions, but think how much bread that twenty-five dollars could buy." The statement was like throwing ice water in Renee's face. She caught her breath, whirled around and walked away from me before I could take back my statement. I felt terrible. *It was cruel of me to have made such a statement,* I thought. Who was I to judge another person? I knew I had ruined a good friendship.

I didn't see Renee for several days, so I wasn't sure if she had used the state pay for the coveted half-pill. I felt miserable. Finally, Renee joined me at a table in the lobby, looking sheepish. I hugged her without asking about her decision—it was none of my business. She volunteered the information, anyway. Renee had not bought the pill.

She said, "You were right, Lucy. It will buy a lot of bread."

It's been ten years since I've seen Renee, but she still writes and lets me know that she still hasn't done drugs, although tempted. She always thinks about how much bread the cost of the drugs will buy. Renee and her son now visit the duck pond often. She continues to thank me for reminding her of what that one moment of weakness almost cost her.

Lucy Serna Killebrew

Thirty-Seven Years in the Wilderness:
A Letter to God

Associate yourself with men of good quality if you esteem your own reputation; for tis better to be alone than in bad company.

George Washington

Dear God:

When I was a child, I felt so alone not having a father around to talk to or other kids my age to play with me. No one wanted to hear my lonely voice. I was always told to go outside and play.

But as usual, there was no one to play with me other than the dirt and wind. I wanted so badly what most kids had—a father. I spent many days in the front yard of our little house hoping that whomever my father was and wherever he was, he would come home to me. Well, he never came home. I guess he just didn't want to or need me as much as I wanted and needed him. I wanted to tell Mama how lonely I felt, but she was always sick and unable to talk to me. *Lord, why did loneliness hurt so bad?*

When I was eleven years old, Mama couldn't afford to

buy me a bicycle, so I borrowed one. Although they said I stole it, I just wanted to know what it was like to ride a bicycle for the first time in my life. I didn't mean to be gone so long. But when they found me, I really felt sad because they said, "Boy, look at you, stealing already. You will never amount to anything. Now take that bike back where you got it." *Lord, why didn't they understand that I only wanted to be loved?*

In junior high school, I didn't have real nice clothes and extra spending money like most other kids. But I stayed away from trouble and made good grades. Because of my raggedy clothes, they all laughed at me and treated me as if I were some kind of disease. There was one teacher, Mrs. Stevens, who must have sensed my loneliness. She treated me nice and always seemed to really care about me. I will always remember the day that she gave me a book and said, "Kenneth, I brought you this, and I want you to read it. One day you are going to be just like the man in this book." The man that she was referring to was Booker T. Washington. Mrs. Stevens was like a mother to me. Because of the concern and love she showed towards me, I wanted to stay in junior high school forever, so I could be near her. But, that was not to be. *Lord, thank you for special angels like Mrs. Stevens.*

The emotional happiness that I had found in the friendship of Mrs. Stevens was short-lived. Three weeks later, the school principal, Mr. Wynn, approached me and said that he needed to talk with me in his office. Mr. Wynn, at six-feet, five-inches and two-hundred-plus pounds, was a formidable figure who created fear in the hearts of those he approached. He always carried a wooden paddle around with him.

When we entered his office, he looked at me with sadness in his eyes and said, "Kenneth, I just received a call from your grandfather. Your mother died this morning."

Mama was born with a hole in her heart, and I didn't get to spend much time with her or around her. She was always sick or in the hospital. And when Mr. Wynn told me that she had died, all I felt was anger and pain—anger because I didn't have a father, and pain because I couldn't understand why Mama left me too. *Lord, help us to accept those things that we don't always understand.*

After Mama's death, things just weren't the same. Before her death, I was just a lonely person. After she died, I became very bitter and hostile. In high school, everybody was so different than me—they were happy and had many friends. I was sad, alone and bitter. School became a place where I no longer wanted to be. I dropped out of school and started hanging around different places smoking marijuana. I wanted to believe that those funny-looking cigarettes would cure my pains of loneliness and anger. But the truth is, they only fueled the fire within me. Soon, my life started falling apart, piece by piece. Everyone except me knew that I was on the path to self-destruction. *Lord, teach us to love one another and help us to understand that we are born with the capacity to heal all the hurts that come our way.*

Well, Lord, thirty-seven years have passed since I first started my journey in the wilderness of life. Although I have been in prison for fifteen of those years, things have changed. You see, Lord, in the eyes of the world, I am nobody, but to you, I am somebody. I want to thank you, with all my heart and soul, for taking this nobody and molding him into somebody—a somebody of conscience, compassion and love for humankind. I thank you for the blessing of special friends, who have inspired me to always be the very best that I can be. Thank you, Lord, for humbling me. Thank you for teaching me that there is no greater love that cures our hurt and pain than your love.

Kenneth L. Bonner
Submitted by Diane Goodhart and Margueritte Hubbard

Brainwashed

Everything is created twice—first mentally, then physically.

Greg Anderson

A prisoner convicted of a minor drug offense completed his time and was ready to go home. The time had come for him to appear at a hearing in front of the parole board to determine if he was ready to be released. Prisoners sit alone across a table from three to four people dressed in suits, and they are grilled, sometimes harshly and provocatively, to test their ability to handle themselves under pressure. The board has the immediate power to send the inmate home or back to their cell for usually ninety days or more before they see the board again for another try. This is one of the most stressful times in a prisoner's life. A failure to please the board is cause for much harassment by fellow prisoners, and in addition, families are disappointed and most times think that the prisoner has messed up in prison and not learned his lesson.

This particular young man was a member of a notorious Los Angeles gang who had been taught to meditate in prison. He practiced diligently every day for eight months. He also completed a forty-day, thirty-one-minute-per-day, powerful mental and physical concentration exercise. This specific and ancient yoga posture technique is said to break any addiction cycle.

In response to the board's questioning, the young man explained to them about his experience in prison and what he learned. He answered, "Through my practices of meditation, and along with my Muslim prayers, I have seen a new path for my life."

A particularly stoic board member shot back at the young man, "So, you have been brainwashed!" as if she were attacking him. The prisoner took a long, slow and even breath and answered, "Yes, ma'am, my brain needed some washing."

The parole board accepted his answer. After his release, the young man enrolled in college and took courses so that he could eventually counsel the troubled youth in his 'hood, thus giving back to his community what was freely given him in prison.

Dan Millstein

Brother Harry

Meditation brings wisdom; lack of meditation leaves ignorance. Know well what leads you forward and what holds you back, and choose the path that leads to wisdom.

Buddha

Harry was an old smuggler, an "around the world one too many times" kind of guy. He was diagnosed with lung cancer a few years ago, but never went for treatment and never stopped smoking. I'd bet he had a few children around the world. He wasn't the happiest kind of guy either, a fault-finder extraordinaire. And now he was doing time for a few packages he had brought into the country from the Far East.

Harry says he never did anything like that before, but the judge didn't care too much and gave him ten years. Harry also said that he only did the smuggling because he needed money for his cancer treatment.

Harry showed up one morning to a meditation class in prison. One could tell he was both articulate and skeptical based on his questioning of the value of meditation.

Harry was fifty years old. With all of his vast worldly experience, he had never had much interest in spiritual matters, psychology, art or religion.

His prognosis was not good, another year to live at best. He would never see the outside world again. Harry would die in prison.

Harry took to meditation quickly. In fact, he became one of those "born-again meditators"—evangelistic, dragging any other prisoner who would listen to him to our Saturday meditation group. "You gotta do this stuff" was Harry's new mantra. Some of the guys were frustrated because of Harry's manic ravings about how he was thinking and feeling due to his new meditation practice.

Harry became somewhat of a celebrity. "Brother Harry" was his new nickname on the yard. He brought new people to every class and kept on them about continuing their own meditation practice. He was becoming quite a guru. Harry was close to death and in prison, yet free for the first time in his life, so he said and so it seemed. Harry was one happy camper.

Now it's not too smart to enjoy yourself in prison. Some of the punishment-type staff people resent you. After all, they can go home after their shift, and many of them are not happy. Why should you, the prisoner, be happy? One of those correctional officers took that very position when it came to Harry.

This officer took exception to Harry's newfound happiness and decided to prove to Harry that prison was far from Disneyland—the happiest place on Earth. At every opportunity, he shook Harry down against the wall two or three times per shift. He would dump Harry's locker contents on to Harry's bunk while he was at breakfast. The officer left Harry's meager goods on display for other inmates to pilfer. Pens, stamps, socks, soaps—all the hard-to-replace stuff was left unsecured. Brother Harry's happy feeling was the cause of him being harassed constantly.

Brother Harry could take a lot; after all, he had nothing more to lose except his newfound inner peace. Harry was fond of saying, "No knuckle-dragging guard was going to take that away from me."

One day the officer was waiting outside the bathroom. As Harry emerged the officer said, "Hands behind your back, we're going for a UA" (urine analysis drug test). Brother Harry knew he was clean and had no worries. This presented another problem though, and Harry protested that he had just gone to the bathroom and would probably not be able to fill a jar for a while.

"Too bad. You fill the jar in the allotted time, or you get written up for no cooperation and get sent to the hole for sixty days."

Harry protested again, "I also have an enlarged prostate gland, and I sometimes have trouble even when I have to go."

"Too bad," the officer grumbled. Harry could not produce and was sent to the hole.

Almost two months later Harry entered the classroom again. This time he was no longer fifty years old, no longer weathered or beat down. Brother Harry had been reborn. He shined like a light. He had a twinkle in his eyes that you could see from across the room. Everyone in the room turned and looked at Brother Harry. He had a few sheets of poetry he wanted to read to everyone. He said, "Fifty-eight days and fifty-eight nights meditating in the hole gave me a great gift. I have my life back. I know I am healed of my cancer, and I am ready to die at the same time. I have been forgiven and have felt the power of God's love for me." He added, "If I can find it, you can too." Brother Harry was back.

One of the guys laughed and said, "Harry, you clean up real good."

The officer who had harassed Harry was transferred while Harry was in the hole. Too bad because Brother Harry wanted to thank him.

Harry has served his time and ten years later is still cancer free. One of the ironies is that Harry had turned to smuggling in an attempt to pay for his cancer treatment. His prayer was answered.

Dan Millstein

Days of Diamonds, Days of Stones

*The gem cannot be polished without friction,
nor man perfected without trial.*

Confucius

As an inmate, I learned early that being slightly crazy is a helpful attribute, since life behind bars is craziness incarnate. After my release and pardon and later in my call to prison ministry, I discovered all truth is relative and loyalty is negotiable. The inmates in power define common sense, logic and reason. They put two and two together and come up with twenty-two. The value of life is linked to the commodity of cigarettes; on a high-stock day, mere existence is worth a pack.

In prison parlance the chaplain is called "Sky Pilot," in reference to our angel missions of messaging, confronting, guidance and comfort. Some of the older staff call us "Padre." Other times we are referred to affectionately as "The Rev."

My days vary. Much like the country song, some days are diamonds and some are stones. On a stone day, I've carried a bloody, unconscious inmate to the nursing station after he'd been beaten up by a stream of angry inmates. A diamond day would see me at a hearing as a deserving prisoner wins parole. I've shared a beer with guards who have unburdened their disillusionment with, ironically, the administration or colleagues—not the inmates.

If I'm dealing with a prisoner experiencing self-pity, I'll send them straight to Scripture. The short list of early murderers, rapists, liars and thieves includes Cain, Noah, Abraham, Esau, Jacob, Rebekah, Moses, David, Solomon, Jezebel, Herod, Pilate, Judas, Peter and Paul. Like us, each one was a mix of saint and sinner. Will D. Campbell wrote in *Brother to a Dragonfly*, "We're all bastards, but God loves us anyway."

I'm old-fashioned enough to distribute copies of Norman Vincent Peale's *The Power of Positive Thinking;* I endorse all of Billy Graham's writings. When I unleash something vicious in chapel, my sermon will be peppered with illustrations about Johnny Cash, Helen Keller or Sister Helen Prejean. I wish to inspire and instill hope.

I don't bring a throw-away-the-key message. Some call prisons "Holiday Inns." I know that is an inaccurate, rude and ignorant statement. Prisons are lonely, fearful and violent places. The loss of freedom can never be under-estimated. A prison cell is about the size of the washroom in an average home, and it's not uncommon to see two or three inmates bunked together. The pacing they do there parallels a hamster running on its wheel to nowhere.

I embrace justice, which works toward restoring one to God, self and community, including one's victim. I abhor prisoners' rights groups that view all prisoners as mis-understood saints, and all guards as unrepentant sadists. I learned from personal experience as a prisoner that I would rather be caught with a knife by a guard than by another prisoner without one.

One elderly inmate from Greece, suffering from Alzheimer's, would drop by my office when he remembered where it was. A thick accent and his illness made for challenging sessions. On a hunch, I brought in a Nana Mouskouri tape of Greek songs. We sat and listened and he cried and cried tears of repentance, lost health and homesickness. When I'd teasingly call him Zorba, he'd laugh. We found a Greek Orthodox priest to visit him, and he found spiritual reconnection. He's in the appropriate hospital now.

One sixties leftover, whose mind was long since burnt, used to listen to Lynyrd Skynyrd and Bad Company tapes, as he told me, "When I look in the mirror, all I see are tombstones in my eyes." We tried to erase that image by helping him reconnect with a daughter he hadn't seen in ten years. A twenty-minute telephone conversation and a later visit helped him finally bury those tombstones.

An old "heavy" known for his fighting skills had become debilitated through illness and was feeling very vulnerable. He said, "I feel like my holster is empty." He relinquished his tough-guy role, and I helped him explore how to be tough in tender ways. This fallen champ later gathered support from other inmates to canvass for the Children's Wish Foundation to benefit terminally ill children.

Crime is ugly and evil, and I don't believe in nonviolent crime or victimless crime. There are no noble outlaws. Although many cheer for the bank robber or Brinks bandit when no one is killed or assaulted, it's no indication of the moral rightness of those crimes.

I minister toward a spiritual awakening and then guide to spiritual development. A prison chaplain must be alert to fanaticism, the dispensation of cheap grace and religious addiction. True rehabilitation comes only through honesty and brutal self-examination. The enemy is within, and that's where the 180-degree turn begins. *Dr. Jekyll and Mr. Hyde* still reads well in a prison cell. Restoration involves full admission of wrongdoing, acknowledgment of who was damaged by our crime and restitution where possible. We must recognize our shadow side and its capacity for destruction, and get in touch with our emotions. This can only be achieved if trust is established, because the pain is so intense, the fury so alive and the crust around the feelings so hardened.

I encourage prisoners to start living the Gospel they claim. That's risky business in prison; it asks if one will continue to step over a stabbed inmate, or maintain silence if a friend is assaulted or murdered. It's a razor's-edge walk of faith, as it recognizes the heart is both bullet-proof and fragile. True discipleship is a humanizing factor behind prison walls.

The best prison chaplains have undertaken the same process, as "all have sinned and fall short of the glory of God." They've met the criminal nature within themselves and they've lost any savior complex. They laugh at how they've been shafted, find a supportive community and are spiritually grounded. They minister under the awareness that a simple, honest mistake can be fatal. They've likely told God more than once they want out, only to hear about sacrifice in a bitter cup. Compassion fatigue plagues most prison chaplains; family, friends, vacations, retreats and prayer are absolutely indispensable. I find a little time off for *bad* behavior is very rejuvenating.

At its best, the prison chapel is a sanctuary and the prison chaplain a voice of conscience. The best prison ministry is delivered by those prison chaplains, visiting spiritual leaders and volunteers with no axe to grind. They're seasoned veterans and eager rookies called by God to proclaim through word and deed, "The Lord sets prisoners free." It is the Christ—once prisoner and death-row chaplain—ministering to two thieves in his dying breath that we so inadequately emulate.

Rod Carter

The Great Escape

Both tears and sweat are salty,
but they render a different result.
Tears will get you sympathy;
sweat will get you change.

Jesse Jackson

I have escaped from prison more times than I can count, thanks to my passion for reading books. Near the beginning of my incarceration at the Federal Correctional Institution in Tucson, Arizona, I came upon a story that deeply affected me.

In 1923, in a small Mississippi town, fifteen-year-old Richard Wright, who was to become one of the most renowned authors in American literature, walked into the local library and handed the librarian a note. It read: "Please let this nigger boy have the following books, Dreiser's *Jennie Gerhardt*, Dostoyevsky's *Poor People*, and Tolstoy's *War and Peace*."

What the librarian didn't know, and young Wright hoped she wouldn't discover, was that he had forged the note himself. He did this in order to use the library card a white friend had loaned him. As the librarian went to get the books, the nervous adolescent looked around the library. He saw an endless abundance of books on the shelves and reading tables. Wright thought to himself, *What joy to be free to browse among all these books at one's leisure—to dig in this volume or that volume, as one has a mind to.*

As I read that story from Wright, it resonated deep within me. I realized that even in this small prison library, I also had the freedom to dig. I no longer had as big a selection as is contained in most libraries on the outside, in any bookstore or on the Internet, but there were still hundreds of books to choose from.

Through the magic provided by books, I no longer have to lay on my narrow bunk with severe restrictions on my movement or schedule. Instead, I can fly to the Middle East on a secret peace mission for my government, walk along the hills and valleys of eighteenth-century New England, or fall in love and raise a family in Paris. Books have always been my passport to enrich both my mind and spirit, but now they are essential to my emotional survival.

Any book can lift me out of my confined existence. The best ones are those where I vanish into the pages, moved by the author's language and imagination. The ultimate thrill is to read something that inspires me to sit down and write. These are the books that stimulate an idea or emotion within me, the ones I want to copy whole paragraphs from, so I can ponder the words at my leisure. For instance, *Chicken Soup for the Soul* books tell how other people have transcended difficulty and inspired themselves and others.

Books have illuminated my life with settings that are familiar to me. In one amazing week, I read Richard Bach's *The Bridge Across Forever*, which switches locales between Florida and California, two states where I spent most of my adult life; *Code 211 Blue*, a police procedural by Joseph

D. McNamara, which takes place in San Francisco, where I lived most recently; and *Angel of Death* by Jack Higgins, which takes place in London, where I spent most of 1984 and 1985 doing seminars and falling in love with that cosmopolitan paradise. For me, reading is not escaping from reality, but choosing an enhanced reality in which to live.

One of the most precious gifts I can give to a fellow prisoner is to share my passion for books. A great satisfaction during my incarceration has been awakening some of the African-American prisoners to their own literary heritage through earlier black writers like Richard Wright and James Baldwin. Sharing some of the moments connected with books can make life more tolerable in some pretty intolerable conditions.

In my first year of incarceration, I read over three hundred books. My favorites were mysteries and self-help books, but I also enjoyed diving into a hearty diet of biographies, classical literature and poetry.

In this most unfamiliar place, I stay in touch with the familiar. Through the magic of reading, I often have the feeling of coming home, returning to a place where I felt loved and welcomed.

Jerry Gillies

Change Is Possible

When you are kind to others, it not only changes you—it changes the world.

Rabbi Harol Kushner
When Bad Things Happen to Good People

Once I was a man who perceived himself, and was perceived by others, as a "loser," an outcast . . . a loner who didn't fit into the normal world of friends, family and happiness. I was a man who had adjusted to a world where stealing, hustling or some other form of violence was the only way of life.

For eighteen years my world and my society revolved around prisons and illegal activities. I had been shot; escaped from a maximum-security prison; and involved in hunger strikes, protests, riots and all kinds of manipulation of the system. Eventually, I became a leader in the negative world of prisons.

Whenever I was released from prison, I felt out of place, an alien in the outside world. I didn't see change as possible and felt I was destined to die a "con." I had become a product of the prison environment.

In those early years, I felt as if God had erred in my construction, as if he had somehow left a component out of me. Deep down inside, I wanted to belong, to be a part of the other world—the world of a white house, picket fence, children and unselfish love that I knew existed out there somewhere. I didn't believe it was possible for me. I truly felt that I couldn't become an honest, loving person. In my mind, change was not an option.

Today, I am a respected leader in my field, a caring father and a loving husband. I am the president of a highly esteemed, reputable corporation, and the proud owner of that cozy white house, complete with picket fence.

What was the secret that eluded me for years and made my life difficult and miserable? How did I find that "other" person inside of me? It wasn't a religious revelation or thunderbolt from heaven. God, in his infinite wisdom, allowed me to recognize that I had the ability to free the "other" person who lay dormant inside me for many years.

The process of change involved my myriad of experiences—some traumatic, some involving just the simple acceptance of the truth. The love and trust of a wife and three beautiful children opened new doors for me. People saw potential for my growth and offered me opportunities to develop that potential, giving me hope and encouragement. These people ranged in positions from lawyers to wardens, bankers to business executives, and real estate brokers to military leaders. They all gave me a chance and saw in me what I could be, not what I had been. Without their support I might still be number 28203.

Gordon Graham

A Simple Witness

I can't change the many years of yesterday,
but I can do something about my tomorrows.

Jackie Kucera

In the summer of 1990, thirty-nine inmates graduated from the first Kairos Prison Ministry Weekend in Ohio. Kairos (meaning God's special time) is a prison ministry that offers a weekend of spiritual awakening to prisoners in higher-security institutions, followed by a continued ministry presence in the form of weekly prayer-and-share groups, monthly reunions and semiannual retreats. It was held at Lebanon Correctional Institution, north of Cincinnati, a close-security facility. That weekend I met inmate Don, and it served as an awakening of my call to ministry to the incarcerated. To say that Don had a profound and life-changing experience is an understatement.

Shortly after his weekend, Don received a ten-year "flop." It would be that long before he could go before the parole board again. His reaction was, "God must have something for me to do here!" One example of his change is reflected in an experience that Don had as the clerk for the Residential

Treatment Unit in R Block, where those requiring separation and psychological medication are housed.

Don was processing paperwork one morning when he saw a movement order for Kenny, an inmate. Kenny had been in prison for a while, and, as far as anyone knew, had never spoken a word to anyone. The movement order was to the Forensic Hospital, a facility for long-term psychiatric care. The paperwork told Don that the next day would be Kenny's birthday. So Don asked the lock officers if it would be possible to give Kenny some time outside of his cell in the open area of the block that next day. Since Kenny had never been a physical problem, the officers agreed to let Kenny sit in a chair for a while. Don then made Kenny a birthday card telling him that God loved him. The other inmate workers and the staff signed the card.

When Kenny's birthday arrived the next day, the officers led him out of his cell to sit in a chair in the open area of the block. Don walked over to him and said, "Happy birthday, Kenny," and laid the birthday card in his lap. The inmate workers and the correctional officers spontaneously began to sing "Happy Birthday to You." The inmates walked up and placed candy bars in Kenny's lap as gifts. Kenny sat there with a tear or two on his cheek. As he opened the card, out fell a Bible tract that Don had put in the card for him.

The next morning, as Kenny was being packed out for his ride to the hospital, one of the correctional officers saw something sticking out of his shirt pocket and asked, "Hey, Kenny, what 'cha got there?"

To everyone's surprise Kenny looked up, pulled the Bible tract out of his pocket and spoke the first words anyone in the institution ever heard him say: "I'm taking my friend Jesus with me."

Chaplain Dick Swan

The Lion and the Mouse

Little friends may prove great friends.

Aesop

In 1988, I attended a Bill Glass Crusade at Angola Prison. Inmates and visitors ate lunch together that day, and I noticed the angry posture of one inmate. He sat nearby with his head down and shoulders slumped. I asked him what was wrong, and he said, "You were the judge who sentenced me to twenty-five years for armed robbery, that's what's wrong."

I started to answer, then hesitated. This was one of the few times in my career on the bench that I was speechless. Other inmates told him he was lucky; one was serving ninety-nine years and another seventy-five years for the same offense. The lowest time sentenced among the others was sixty years. They told Omar to thank me for the twenty-five years, and I appreciated the other inmates sticking up for me. Omar obviously didn't agree. He said nothing else.

Ten years later, I judged a speech contest and was

impressed with one inmate from Hunt Prison who made an outstanding presentation. I approached him, as he was smiling and joking with other inmates, and we spoke for several minutes about his presentation. During the conversation, he asked if I remembered him. I looked at this happy young man, who spoke eloquently but couldn't remember meeting him.

He reminded me of our confrontation in 1988. I couldn't believe the transformation. While serving his time, Omar had gotten involved in a group to improve his speaking skills, received his GED, and learned to repair and upgrade computer equipment. Since the sentence I had given him was relatively short, he was able to reduce it to half the time.

When he was released, Omar called me. He was having trouble finding a job since people are reluctant to hire former armed robbers. Our ethics code prohibits judges from giving letters of recommendation to people who have not worked for us directly. Omar agreed to do some volunteer work for me, so I could give him a letter of recommendation.

Our staff was racing against time to make all our computers Y2K compliant, so I sent Omar to help them. He was so helpful that they asked to keep him. Hunt Prison had done a great job teaching him about computers.

Omar agreed to work even though I told him I couldn't guarantee that the other judges would agree to pay him. One of the judges had been his public defender. Naturally, not many of the judges were very excited about having an armed robber work on our computers, but he did such a great job that they all voted to pay Omar for his work. This was especially wonderful since it was just before Christmas.

Later, I was able to recommend Omar to another firm that rehabilitated computers for schools, and he landed a permanent job there. It was like the fable of *The Lion and the Mouse.* The lion had no idea that the mouse whose life he spared could later save his life. I thought that I was just helping Omar out, but instead he helped bring us through the Y2K problem without a glitch.

Judge Bob Downing

If you treat prisoners well, they will be less angry, less inclined to violence inside prison, less likely to provoke violent actions by guards, less likely to have reason to file brutality lawsuits that cost taxpayers a bundle and waste administrators' time. And most important, well-treated prisoners will be less likely to leave prison angrier, more vicious and more inclined to criminal behavior than when they went in.

Frank Wood
Former Commissioner of Corrections, Minnesota
Reprinted by permission of Charles Carkhuff.

Writing Can Change the World

The power of words inspires the power for change.

Mary Kay Kurzweg

Howard's story is one of many soul-inspiring accounts of inmate triumph over utter desolation. As a child, his home was an alcoholic battlefield. His God was a God of retribution. Young Howard sensed that he had already been banished to a world of demons and devils. In his nightmares he ran from monsters. Reality was a rude awakening, and he eventually ran away from home. In the shadowy jungle of inner-city streets, the homeless teen battled with an untreated manic-depressive disorder. He soon turned to alcohol and street drugs, which temporarily relieved the mental anguish. As the vicious cycle of addiction took hold, his unbearable condition worsened to the point that Howard contemplated suicide.

Local libraries served as an oasis from the dangerous streets and offered the young man a sense of security. There, among thousands of published volumes, Howard spent hours escaping into the easy-reading, inspirational stories he enjoyed. These stirring accounts, by authors such as Dr. Norman Vincent Peale and Billy Graham, provided Howard with moments of authentic hope.

As the seasons passed, Howard grew into adulthood. He made contact with his mother, who had divorced, stopped drinking and worked hard to give Howard's younger brothers the chance he didn't have. She became a loving mother for Howard and his strongest supporter. Howard's reading improved, and he aspired to write like the many motivational authors he read. His nights were spent in missions, shelters or on the street. Days were used to scratch literary passages, including poetry, onto sheets from library notepads. As Howard remained in collision with cycles of manic and depressive states, his desire to maintain meaningful employment and a normal life was to no avail.

Paralyzing anxiety and despair were his lot in life. Howard's mother tried desperately to help her son, who was losing touch with reality. Ultimately, however, his menacing bipolar mood swings, aggravated by drug abuse, led the desperate man to steal money to "medicate" himself. Howard's dreams of writing for publication and living a rational life were shattered the moment he handed a bank teller a note directing her to hand over bank money. Fleeing the scene on foot, he cursed himself for what he had done.

Howard accepted responsibility for his regrettable action. In court, a federal district judge sentenced a dejected Howard to five years in the federal system. As he peered through the metal bars, life appeared bleak. He doubted he would ever have a life.

Three years later, with the assistance of prison medical staff, Howard succeeded in his ongoing treatment for the bipolar disorder. His rehabilitation has been remarkable. Howard has authored dozens of inspirational stories and hundreds of contemporary verses. By taking advantage of the prison's Interlibrary Book Loan Program, he studied, focused and became accomplished in the publishing business. Howard has had his literary works accepted for publication in international magazines, anthologies, newsletters and online publications.

Having earned his GED diploma, he is currently a college sophomore with a major in anthropology. Howard has achieved numerous certificates for courses in drug abuse prevention, anger management, computer literacy, world history, life skills and creative writing. Howard was a GED writing skills tutor for the education department at a Texas federal correctional facility. He received an early release in January 2000 and is contributing much to society.

"I hope that somehow my writings help others in need of a spiritual lift," Howard explains. "God whom I once thought disfavored me, has changed my life. With the gift he has given me—to create meaningful literary work—I aspire to share this with others. Our writing can change the world!"

Tony Webb

A Magic Touch

The universe is full of magical things patiently waiting for our wits to grow sharper.

Eden Phillpots

Part of the satisfaction for any teacher is seeing the light go on when a student is able to grasp a new concept. It's no different for those of us who happen to teach incarcerated adults.

I used to constantly drill my seventh and eighth grade academic class on the merits of honesty when it came to taking tests. I would remind them that, "Cheaters never win, and winners never cheat." Many times this admonition would illicit boos and snickers, but I would repeat it anyway, and remind them that when they cheated, they weren't cheating me—only themselves.

As I sat grading a language test that required using simple, compound and complex sentences, I noticed that two of my adult inmate-student papers had the exact same sentences. I didn't intend to make a big scene out of it, so I simply wrote on each paper, "My, your answers are exactly the same as Mr. _____'s. When you decide to rely on your own intelligence, you will begin to amaze yourself." Once I made my comments and returned the papers to the class, I didn't give the incident another thought.

Moments after returning to my desk and beginning another stack of paperwork, an irate student jumped up from his desk in the full heat of anger. It took me a moment to realize what was going on and another moment to zero in on what he was saying. By then, he was at my desk hovering over me with his paper in hand. He not only had my attention, but the entire class was frozen in anticipation of what was going to happen next.

At our institution, all staff are required to carry whistles, and those working directly with inmates must wear personal alarms at all times. I could sense immediately that the rest of the class was waiting for me to push my alarm due to this impending threat of great bodily harm.

Once an alarm is sounded, within seconds, a full complement of custody officers is on hand to deal with the situation by whatever means are necessary. It's also understood that all inmates must stop where they are and either sit in their seats or on the floor if no seat is available. They must not in any way impede the movement of custody officers to the scene of the alarm.

Knowing this, my class became as quiet as those proverbial church mice. It was so quiet I could hear a heartbeat—mine! The entire situation seemed surreal and almost as though I were having an out-of-body experience. I listened to this middle-aged man's nonstop ranting.

Both he and I knew that all attention was squarely focused on us. All were waiting to see how the performance would play out. They already knew I would win because I automatically had the upper hand. But, what would winning cost me? A staff assault? Embarrassment? A shouting match? Humiliation and a weakened base of authority? Regardless, I was not prepared to pay the price. In a situation such as this, it's imperative to maintain control without compromising the trusting relationship I had built with the other students.

After reflecting on this student I thought I knew well, I looked at him with a smile, gently placing the palm of my hand under his chin. "Unclench those jaws before you address me, Mister," I said without yelling. It wasn't a threat. In an instant, the student melted into a stick of butter, and everyone was laughing, including him. In the next breath, he apologized and said he was sorry for yelling. Then he admitted cheating and felt bad for getting caught. He said, "Gee, Ms. Carter, not only did I get caught cheating, but then I had the nerve to make you prove it to me." He vowed never to do it again.

I could almost hear the whoosh of air as the other students breathed a sigh of relief. I could see the light of recognition in his eyes over the lesson he had just taught himself. All it took was a magic touch that transmitted more than I realized. It put everyone else "on notice" that I was *for* them—not *against* them.

Toni Carter

My Defining Moment

The ultimate measure of a man is not where he stands in moments of comfort and convenience, but where he stands at times of challenge and controversy.

Dr. Martin Luther King Jr.

Who would have ever thought that I would find one of my most life-defining moments in a prison? At the age of forty-four, I decided to take a job as a business administrator in a local prison full of rapists, murderers, arsonists, drug dealers and mobsters. Most of my friends thought I was nuts, and even my husband, who loved me and totally supported my career, had some reservations about my decision.

Though I harbored some doubts myself, I went into my new career with the attitude that I would have little to do with the actual inmates. After all, my job was making sure the budget was in line, nothing more. Yet once on the job, the warden explained that she expected me to make rounds—to go out among the inmates to ensure their needs were being met. So much for staying safe within my office.

I did as she asked with a great deal of discomfort. I would go home at night with my stomach churning. *What was I doing in a prison? I don't belong here.* When I arrived at work each day, I would hear the steel doors slam shut behind me—not once—but twice. *I am in here with them. What if they hurt me? Or kill me? I may not go home tonight and be with my husband again. Why did I take this job?*

Several months later, the warden approached me again, and this time said she wanted me to facilitate an inmate program. I questioned my ability to do as she asked, but if she had such faith in me, surely I should have the same faith in myself. The prison school administrator and I began teaching the Gaining Opportunity and Living Skills, or GOALS Program, to the inmates, in hopes of teaching them the tools and skills needed to increase their self-esteem and begin to feel good about themselves.

I began teaching the class and appeared cool, calm and collected. As nervous as I was, I felt I presented myself very professionally. In the course of the program, I came to know what making a difference in someone's life really meant. I learned from the inmates that life is very different for each of us, and that everyone has burdens to bear. I had believed my life tragedies and sorrows were enough, but when I heard them describe their lifetimes of pain and hurt, I began to explore my own true spirit. I saw men with horrible pasts, years' worth of pain and hurt inside them, remorseful for what they had done, and angry at what had happened to them in life; and I was sitting in the room amongst them. And in the midst of their pain, hurt, crying, and sharing, I began to learn something about myself. As this revelation became clearer to me, I would ask myself, *"How do you know when you have made a difference in someone's life?"* The answer still wasn't exactly clear and defined for me, but it was coming.

A few months passed and as I got more involved in the

programming and rehabilitative aspects of prison management, I began to change my thoughts. I began to see many inmates are respectful human beings, trying to make positive changes in their lives, willing to work at being a better person. They yearned to go home to their families. I saw them perform in Easter and Christmas plays, which was a forum for them to display their wonderful talents; I heard them sing of their love for God, and express their spirit in positive ways; I saw them sew quilts, train pilot dogs, cry when the parole board left, and cry when their parents died. I arranged funeral visits, and felt an inmate's pain when he went to see his father for the last time. I heard him say "thank you" to me for making the arrangements. I was on duty when another inmate committed suicide, and I had to tell the family members. Having lost my own beautiful child of nineteen years, I shared their ache of losing a child.

I realized that this was life, and I was caught in the middle of it. *Could this be where God planned for me to be? Am I making a difference? Is my life being defined in some way each day in this prison with these gentlemen?*

One day while sitting in the chapel watching Warden Christine Money teach sign language to sixty inmates, I watched as I listened to the song, "You Are the Wind Beneath My Wings." They passionately used their fingers and hands to demonstrate their love, and I realized, sitting in the middle of them, looking into their eyes, and hearing the music and words, that I was exactly where I was supposed to be in my life. I felt as though I was living the plan that was designed for me, and it finally dawned on me in that moment. The revelation was now clear. I had not made as much of a difference in their lives, as they had made a difference in mine.

I realized that some of those men thought like me, believed like me, hoped like me, breathed like me, cried like me, and their hearts hurt like mine when pain strikes. At times confusion would amass my thoughts, and prayer directed me to do the right thing. I knew I had an opportunity. Then, one day while reaching deep within my soul, I realized *I was receiving and giving a gift at the same time in a place I never imagined.* I had to be open to receive it and accept who I was in all my frailties. This was my defining moment.

Through my sharing of my life experiences and talents, these men were being given the gift of learning how to feel better about who they were; and I was receiving a gift I never would have expected—one of spiritual love and compassion from those society had taught me to reject. I witnessed broken lives and watched shattered relationships begin to heal. I saw the pain of family members and the spirit of hope for newness in that healing. My defining moment was found in a most unusual place.

Colleen Fiant

Beneath the Layers of Filth

Being easily identifiable as a Jew in one of Michigan's prisons, isn't always the smartest thing to do since it makes the person a perfect target for every bigot with an attitude. I know. I am an incarcerated Jew who wears a kippah (skullcap), beard and tallit katan (a small undershirt with ritual fringes attached) despite the inevitable heckling such attire draws.

Several years ago, at a weekly Torah study group, the prison's chaplain allowed me to lead. A new participant arrived late—one who I immediately knew wasn't Jewish. In our little group he stood out like a piglet among puppies. It wasn't that our group was exclusively Jewish either. We had men from several other faiths. It was his closely cropped hair and numerous tattoos displaying swastikas and other Nazi-like memorabilia that quieted our group and set him apart from us.

After a moment or two of staring at one another, he dropped his gaze to the carpet and asked in a barely audible voice whether or not he could join us for the evening. To say that I was shocked is an understatement, but I recovered quickly enough so I didn't gawk at him too long before rising and inviting him to take a seat across from me. What followed is something I would never have expected from within a prison's hard, cold walls.

Although it shames me today, I didn't treat Ron very well that first night. I could only see the symbols that had doomed six million of my people to their horrible deaths. Whether following my lead or through revulsion of their own, none of the other members tried to engage Ron in conversation, leaving him very alone in an otherwise crowded room. The next week was a repetition of the first.

Prior to the third session, Ron asked for a minute of the group's time.

"By now you're probably wondering why I'm here," Ron said in his quiet voice, fixing his gaze firmly on the tabletop. "I'm here to change. I'm here to learn how to stop hating others . . . to stop hating myself."

Ron then spent the next half hour pouring out his heart to us about how he'd grown up in a dysfunctional, racist family in California, gotten busted for hate-related burglaries and ended up in some of California's toughest prisons, where he became a fervent member of the Aryan Brotherhood. After earning a delayed parole, Ron came to Michigan to escape his past, only to wind up falling back into his old patterns of behavior—a decision that led to his present incarceration. When Ron finished, he looked up. There were tears flowing down his cheeks. It was at that point that our group was forever changed.

We spent the first portion of each session over the next few months working with Ron, challenging his beliefs and exploring his reasons for wanting to change. It was a difficult task and one that I frequently thought he'd abandon. Ron continued to take great emotional and physical risks to come to terms with the things he'd done.

I knew Ron wasn't the same man I'd first met when he started walking the yard with me—an act that publicly shouted Ron's renunciation of hate to those who once counted him among their bigoted elite. To his credit, Ron silently withstood his ex-friends' taunts and continued seeking new ways to improve himself.

Eventually, when our entire group was satisfied that Ron wasn't pulling some type of elaborate con game, we pooled our money and paid to have Ron's tattoos covered up by one of the prison's best illegal artists. We also put him in touch with several outreach organizations and convinced him to help others who were blindly stumbling down his old path.

Ron had come to our group seeking positive change. He found it. He also became a person I am proud to call a friend. Ron, however, also changed me. He renewed my waning belief in mankind's ability to overcome its senseless hatred—to find its goodness buried beneath layers of encrusted filth. From this one individual, and from within an openly hostile environment, dozens have learned acceptance of that which is different. I will go to my grave knowing few greater accomplishments.

Douglas Burgess

3

ON FAITH

Born with a hard head, I lived by my own rules. My greed and pride kept me believing I couldn't be had and that I didn't need God. The truth is, I was lost and living in a self-made prison of drugs, money and sex . . . a prison much stronger and more debilitating than the physical kind. The real question isn't why I came back to prison, but rather why I wasn't dead. I was so close to hell you could smell the smoke on my clothes. But God in his mercy and love snatched me away from that destiny.

Roy A. Borges

Ivy's Cookies

That's the thing about faith. If you don't have it, you can't understand it. And if you do, no explanation is necessary.

Major Kira Nerys

The clank of the metal door and the echo of their footsteps rang in the ears of Ivy and Joanne as they walked down the dingy corridor behind the prison guard toward the "big room." The aroma of Ivy's homemade chocolate chip cookies wasn't enough to override the stench of ammonia from the recently mopped floor or the bitterness and anger that hung in the air. Women's Correctional Institute was not the kind of place where seventeen-year-olds go for an outing, but Ivy had a mission.

She didn't know what she was getting into, but she had to try. With trembling fingers, she dialed the number for an appointment at the prison. Warden Baylor was receptive to Ivy's desire to visit and referred her to Joanne, another teen who had expressed interest.

"How do we do this?" Ivy asked.

"Who knows? Maybe homemade cookies would break the ice," Joanne suggested.

So they baked their cookies and here they were, bearing gifts to strangers.

"I put almonds in these," Ivy rambled nervously as they moved along. "The dough was gummier than usual. . . ."

"Don't chatter," the guard snapped. "It gets the prisoners riled."

The harsh words made Ivy jump and her heart pound. She walked the rest of the distance in silence.

"Okay. Here we are," the guard grunted, keys rattling. "You go in. I'll lock the door behind you. Be careful what you say. They have a way of using your words against you. You have fifteen minutes. Holler if you have any trouble." Ivy noted the prisoners' orange jumpsuits and felt overdressed. *Maybe we shouldn't have worn heels,* she thought. *They probably think we're snobs.*

Remembering the guard's admonition, the girls put the cookies on the table next to plastic cups of juice without a word. Some prisoners leaned against the wall; others stood around—watching. Studying. Thinking. Staring. Nobody talked. Ivy smiled at one of the women, and she scowled back. From then on, she avoided eye contact. After five minutes of strained silence, Joanne whispered, "Let's move away from the table. Maybe they'll come over."

As they stepped back, one of the prisoners blurted out, "I'm gettin' a cookie." The others followed and began helping themselves. Soon they heard the rattle of keys. Time was up.

"What a relief to get outta there," Joanne sighed as a gust of fresh air caressed their perspiring faces.

"Yeah," Ivy agreed. "But there's a tug inside me that we're not done. Would you be willing to go back?"

Joanne nodded with a half-smile. "How about Thursday after school?"

Week after week they came. And week after week the prisoners ate the cookies, drank the juice and stood around in silence. Gradually, antagonistic looks were replaced by an occasional smile. Still, Ivy couldn't bring herself to speak—not a word.

Then one Thursday, an evangelist walked in. Her step was sure, her chin was high and she glowed with the love of God. But she meant business. "I've come to pray with you," she announced. "Let's make a circle."

Ivy was awed by the inmates' compliance. Only a few resisted. The others, although murmuring, inched their way toward the middle of the room and formed a lopsided circle, looking suspiciously at one another.

"Join hands," the evangelist instructed. "It's not gonna hurt ya, and it'll mean more if you do." Slowly they clasped hands, some grasping hard, others barely touching. "Now, bow your heads." Except for the orange outfits, it could have been a church meeting.

"Okay. We're gonna pray," she continued, "and prayer is just like talking, only to God. I want to hear you tell the Lord one thing you're thankful for. Just speak it out. Don't hold back."

Ivy's palms were sweaty. *I can't pray out loud, Lord. I can't even talk to these women. Guess I should set an example, but they probably don't even like me—think I'm better than them 'cause of my clothes.*

The words of an inmate jolted from her thoughts.

"I'm thankful, God, for Miss Ivy bringing us cookies every week."

Another voice compounded the shock, "God, thanks for bringing a black lady to see us, not just Quakers and Presbyterians."

Ivy's eyes brimmed with tears as she heard, "Thank you, God, for these two ladies givin' their time every week even though we can't do nothin' to pay 'em back."

One by one, every inmate in the circle thanked God for Ivy and Joanne. Then Joanne managed to utter a prayer of gratitude for the prisoners' words. But when it came Ivy's turn, she was too choked up to speak. Her eyes burned in humble remorse over how wrong she'd been about these women. She wished she could blow her nose, but the inmates were squeezing her hands so tightly, she resorted to loud sniffles and an occasional drip.

The following week, Ivy and Joanne returned, bright-eyed, to find the prisoners talkative.

"Why *do* you bring us cookies every week?" a husky voice inquired from the corner of the room. When Ivy explained, she inched a few steps closer. "Can you get me a Bible?" she asked. Others wanted to know more about the Jesus who inspires teenagers to visit prisoners.

A ministry was born from Ivy's cookies. What started as a silent act of kindness turned into a weekly Bible study at the prison that eventually grew so big it split into several groups that continue to this day. After Joanne married and moved away, Ivy continued to minister to the inmates alone for years. Eventually Prison Fellowship picked up the baton.

Ivy is a grandmom now. Her radiance has increased over the years, and she brightens any room she enters. But last Thursday afternoon she indulged herself in a good cry. Curled up on the couch, wrapped in the afghan her daughter had made, she wept. Deep sobs wracked her body as she remembered it had been one year since her daughter died of asthma. She ached over the loss and felt, for the first time, the full weight of her words, "The kids can live with me." The baby was asleep in his crib and the two girls were in school when the doorbell rang.

There stood a young woman, probably seventeen, with a plate of homemade cookies.

"Are you Ivy Jones?" she asked.

"Yes," she answered, dabbing her eyes with a wadded tissue.

"These are for you," the girl said as she handed the cookies to her with a shy, sad smile, turning to leave with-out another word.

"Thank you," Ivy whispered in a daze. The girl was halfway down the sidewalk when Ivy called out, "But why?"

"My grandmother gave me her Bible before she died last week, and her last words were, 'Find Ivy Jones and take her some homemade cookies.'"

As the girl walked away, a wave of precious memories, uncertainties and younger days flooded Ivy's soul. Swallowing the lump in her throat, she choked back a sob and headed toward the phone. *It's been a long time since I talked with Joanne.*

Candy Abbott

THE IN SIDE

Reprinted by permission of Matt Matteo.

Dead Man Walking

It is no use walking anywhere to preach, unless our walking is our preaching.

St. Francis of Assisi

While I was working at a public housing project in New Orleans, I began corresponding with a death row inmate, Patrick Sonnier, at the Louisiana State Penitentiary in Angola.

The hero of my book, *Dead Man Walking*, is Lloyd LeBlanc, the father of one of the two teens who Sonnier was convicted of killing. Lloyd exhibited the love of Jesus Christ in the way he dealt with and prayed for Sonnier.

At one point before Sonnier's execution, Lloyd visited with me and said, "I don't believe in the death penalty. I just want an apology."

When people are in white-hot pain, you don't know what to do. It's such a natural thing for the rage to rise up in us. Good and decent people feel outrage over crime. Time spent with people is the answer to the problem of coming to grips with wrath and bitterness. Maybe the best thing we can give people is our presence. We become the hands, we become the eyes . . . of Jesus. There are some spaces of sorrow that only God can touch. In *Dead Man Walking* I write:

> Lloyd LeBlanc has told me that he would have been content with imprisonment for Patrick Sonnier. He went to the execution, he says, not for revenge, but hoping for an apology. Patrick Sonnier had not disappointed him. Before sitting in the electric chair he had said, "Mr. LeBlanc, I want to ask your forgiveness for what me and Eddie done," and Lloyd LeBlanc had nodded his head, signaling a forgiveness he had already given. He says that when he arrived with sheriff's deputies there in the cane field to identify his son, he had knelt by his boy—"Laying down there with his two little eyes sticking out like bullets"—and prayed the Our Father. And when he came to the words: "Forgive us our trespasses as we forgive those who trespass against us," he had not halted or equivocated, and he said, "Whoever did this, I forgive them." But he acknowledges that it's a struggle to overcome the feelings of bitterness and revenge that well up, especially as he remembers David's birthday year by year and loses him all over again: David at twenty, David at twenty-five, David getting married, David standing at the back door with his little ones clustered around his knees, grown-up David, a man like himself, whom he will never know. Forgiveness is never going to be easy. Each day it must be prayed for and struggled for and won.*

Lloyd is one of the most Christlike people I've ever met. He said that his faith required him to oppose Sonnier's execution. He said, "I know that's the road Jesus wants me to go down."

Sister Helen Prejean, CSJ

Excerpted from Dead Man Walking, *pp. 244 to 245.*

A Wise Old Man

Happiness is a butterfly which, when pursued, is always beyond our grasp, but, if you will sit down quietly, may alight upon you.

Nathaniel Hawthorne

It seemed as if the night would never end. His soul was in a deep sleep, but his mind was still contemplating what seemed so unreal, but was very much his new reality. He tossed the idea poignantly around in his head, but before he could come to a definite conclusion, it was time for him to wake up to a new day. This was the hardest time of day—early mornings that offered no peace of mind. These were subtle beginnings that offered no guarantees, only the constant reminder that tomorrow would be no different from today.

He waited patiently for breakfast to be brought to him, having one more day before he would be placed into the general population. It was hard for Jason to adapt to the fact that prison was now his new home. After breakfast, the guard, who was much smaller than Jason, with a pot-belly and a smile that disarmed heartlessness, gave him an opportunity to go into the courtyard and have a smoke.

Jason slowly inhaled on his cigarette, releasing a cloud of smoke that hovered in the air. To his right was a small bed of flowers that an old man was tending. He had a beard full of gray hair, large eyes from years of looking out into the world and a pleasant, carefree demeanor. He looked up amiably and spoke, "How long have you been here, son?"

Jason noticed that the guard had walked over to a gate and was quietly conversing with a fellow. "Only three days," he answered between puffs. "Hey, that is a pretty impressive garden of flowers you have there."

"Well thanks," said the old man as he got up and walked toward Jason. He took a seat beside him.

"Smoke?" Jason asked, as he offered his pack to his new friend.

"Thanks, but no thanks. It isn't my cup of tea."

"How long have you been here?" Jason asked curiously.

"Oh, I've been in and out for many years," the old man said while laughing and stroking his beard.

"You must like it here," Jason said.

"I like it everywhere. The world is truly a beautiful place."

"I hate this place," Jason responded, "but after tomorrow, I'm a ghost."

The old man stared at Jason with a puzzled look before asking, "Where are you going?"

Jason ignored him because he really had no intention of saying that out loud.

A butterfly landed softly on the petal of a flower. It was black with large yellow and orange ovals on its wings. "Do you think it will be worth it?" the older man asked.

"Worth what?" Jason asked.

"Leaving this world," the old man said. Jason looked at him in silence. He feared if it got back to the guard that he was planning to hang himself in his cell, they would keep him in maximum security.

As if sensing Jason's fear, he said, "It's okay. Your little secret is safe with me and the butterfly. You have my word. You made a mistake and landed in this hellhole, and now you are ready to call it quits?"

"Look here, old man, it's hard enough being a black man as it is. Now my burden is even greater. What kind of future is there for a felon?" Jason exclaimed.

"Son, life is more than titles and records. It's about what is in your heart. People make mistakes every day, and some never get caught, but you were lucky."

"How do you figure that?" asked Jason.

"Because you were caught, and by divine grace you have a second chance. You can use these trials and tribulations to your benefit. You must realize that this is all part of a much greater plan. Persevere, son, because if you could not handle it, you would not be here."

Jason saw the guard heading back his way; the old man went back to tending his garden. The butterfly sat quietly, exquisitely absorbing the sun's rays. The old man whispered to the small creature, and it flew over to Jason, perching on his shoulder as if to say, *Humility and humble beginnings are roots to everlasting grace, so why worry in a world where it has no place? Your extremities are the creator's opportunities. Young man, lift your head to the sky—I used to crawl upon my naked belly, but now I can fly.*

Andre T. Jackson

Never Second Guess God's Ways

Take the first step in faith. You don't have to see the whole staircase, just take the first step.

Martin Luther King Jr.

Just seven days after being freed from prison, I was back again—this time as a visitor. The main reason for that decision was Paul Kramer, a twenty-seven-year-old, ex-marine drug offender—the young man I met my first lonely and frightening night at Maxwell prison. Together we had formed a small Bible study group there. It had grown as God's spirit moved through the prison, and we had become as close as brothers. Leaving Paul behind when I was transferred to Holabird for the last two months of my imprisonment was one of the saddest moments of my time behind bars. Hopefully this visit would provide reassurance, since he still had another year to serve. I wanted Paul to know he was expected in our home when his sentence was up.

To my chagrin I saw that a TV camera crew was set up at the front door of the prison administration building. Being a once-powerful White House official, word had leaked out about my visit. Two blue-jacketed guards escorted me to the familiar open compound, surrounded by the four, one-story, white stucco dormitory buildings. The setting was unchanged from that day many months earlier when I had been ushered in as prisoner #23226.

Then I saw Paul walking toward the glass-sided control room from which all movement inside the prison is monitored. When he saw me, a broad grin spread across his face. He started to jog towards me. Without giving it a thought, I wrapped my arms around him and hugged him warmly.

The cameras had been turning and this irked me. Physical contact between inmates is prohibited in many prisons; any sign of affection is viewed with suspicion in places where homosexual behavior is such a pervasive problem.

"They'll show that on television tonight and half the world will believe we're queer," I lamented to Paul.

"Who cares?" Paul replied, as we walked slowly to the visiting area. "It's all in the Lord's hand."

He was right. Weeks later I learned that a stubborn nonbeliever in western Pennsylvania was alone watching the late news when the footage of Kramer and me greeting each other was flashed on the TV screen. The man later wrote me: "For years I have resisted church in every sermon my wife forced me to listen to. But seeing a once-powerful White House official embracing that poor prisoner got to me somehow as none of the other arguments ever did. I knew Christianity had to be real." He then said that he had become a believer that very night.

I was being taught never to second-guess God's ways.

Charles W. Colson

One Day Outside My Prison Window

One day outside my prison window,
A sparrow came to me.
I asked, "Hey, little sparrow,
How's it feel to be so free?"

He shook his head, as he replied,
"I thought the prisoner was me . . .
For you have the ability to pray
And only prayer can set you free."

Efrain Frank Hernandez

Christmas in Jail
(A Strange Place to Find Peace on Earth)

When the song of the angels is stilled, when the star in the sky is gone, when the kings and princes are home, when the shepherds are back with their flock, the work of Christmas begins: to find the lost, to heal the broken, to feed the hungry, to release the prisoner, to rebuild the nations, to bring peace among brothers, to make music in the heart.

Howard Thurman

When the Mexican teenager walked into the county jail in Newport, Kentucky, he was understandably nervous. The nineteen-year-old, baby-faced Hispanic youth had never been in jail before, and he had no idea what to expect. Would he be robbed, assaulted, raped?

The other prisoners looked at him with suspicion. They distrusted anyone who did not share their anger, paranoia and mindless destructiveness. Zamora had reason to fear them. He was a simple boy from a small mountain town in Mexico who didn't even speak English.

After a few days passed and the terror in his eyes sub-sided, I approached him. I decided to teach Zamora enough English to survive in jail. He grinned when he sensed that I was going to help him. I made flash cards of the alphabet out of toilet paper. He was an eager student and learned the entire alphabet in just two days. But he still didn't have any idea what the words he was learning meant.

A volunteer jail visitor from Exodus brought me an English/Spanish dictionary that I gave to Zamora. With the help of me and the other men in the cell, Zamora soon learned English. He became our mascot and the little brother we all needed.

Zamora asked me to help him learn to read the Bible. I selected the Christmas story in Luke. A week before Christmas, the volunteer church visitors were stunned and joyful as Zamora read the Christmas story in nearly perfect English. Many eyes filled with tears. My own eyes were damp. I was proud of Zamora. At that time it seemed as though I was looking into the innocent face of a young Jesus.

With Christmas a few days away, I wondered what I could give to Zamora to celebrate his new victory. My lawyer brought me a large color picture of Jesus. It was beautiful and even seemed to have Hispanic features. What better way to cement our friendship and celebrate his learning English than to give him this picture? When I looked at that peaceful, beautiful face, I realized what a contrast it was to the fear, hurt and loneliness we experi-ence in jail.

Two days before Christmas, I surprised Zamora with the picture of Jesus. Tears filled his eyes as he accepted this special Christmas gift. It was at that moment I real-ized that he had a family somewhere in Mexico wonder-

ing where he was. His family must have taught him to
love Jesus. We hung the picture on the jailhouse wall, and
all the prisoners seemed pleased.

The day before Christmas, the guards ordered all pictures taken down from the walls. I asked if the picture of
Jesus could be left up through Christmas. The answer was
"No," under threat of additional punishment. Anger in our
cellhouse rose in protest. In spite of the threat of punishment, we all agreed to keep the picture of Jesus on the wall.
To our surprise there was no objection from the guards.

It's typical in jail that, as Christmas Eve arrives, emotions run high and tension mounts as prisoners, deprived
of normal social interaction with loved ones, strike out in
anger and frustration at one another. Even though we still
felt the tension, we also noticed a strange peace in our
own crowded cell. While fights broke out in other cells,
there were none in ours.

Just before bedtime I asked Zamora if he wanted to say
the Lord's Prayer in his beautiful native Spanish. When he
finished, I joined him in saying that beautiful healing
prayer in English. There was no doubt that Christ was
with us that night in jail.

On Christmas morning the picture of Jesus still hung
on our wall. Somehow, now it didn't even matter if they
were to order it removed. After all, wasn't Jesus in our
hearts and actions? All of us had a new appreciation for
the power of love that Jesus represented to us. "Feliz
Navidad," I wished Zamora in my clumsy Spanish.

"Merry Christmas, Lou," he replied in nearly perfect
English. It seemed a strange place for me to find peace on
Earth at Christmas—in a jail cell.

Lou Torok

THE IN SIDE

Perfect Freedom

True joy is claiming the freedom to be who you are.

Marcia Reynolds

As one who has served time in prison and has since spent most of my life working in them, I'll never forget the most unusual prison I've ever visited.

Called Humaita Prison, it is in Sao Jose dos Campos in Brazil. Formerly a government prison, it is now operated by Prison Fellowship Brazil as an alternative prison, without armed guards or high-tech security. Instead, it is run on the Christian principles of love of God and respect for men.

Humaita has only two full-time staff; the rest of the work is done by the 730 inmates serving time for everything from murder and assault to robbery and drug-related crimes. Every man is assigned another inmate to whom he is accountable. In addition, each prisoner is assigned a volunteer mentor from the outside who works with him during his term and after his release. Prisoners take classes on character development and are encouraged to participate in educational and religious programs.

When I visited this prison, I found the inmates smiling—particularly the murderer who held the keys, opened the gates and let me in. Wherever I walked, I saw men at peace. I saw clean living areas. I saw people working industriously. The walls were decorated with motivational sayings and Scripture.

Humaita has an astonishing record. Its recidivism rate is 4 percent, compared to 75 percent in the rest of Brazil. How is that possible?

I saw the answer when my inmate guide escorted me to the notorious cell once used for solitary punishment. Today, he told me, it always houses the same inmate. As we reached the end of the long concrete corridor and he put the key into the lock, he paused and asked, "Are you sure you want to go in?"

"Of course," I replied impatiently. "I've been in isolation cells all over the world." Slowly he swung open the massive door, and I saw the prisoner in that cell: a crucifix, beautifully carved—Jesus, hanging on the cross.

"He's doing time for the rest of us," my guide said softly.

Charles W. Colson

I Was in Prison

The richest spiritual experiences I have ever known have not been in vaulted cathedrals surrounded by stained-glass windows, but in the filthiest prison cells.

Charles Colson

I never thought I would end up in prison, but that's exactly what happened. It began in 1983 when I received a copy of Charles Colson's book, *Loving God*, as a Christmas gift. This collection of powerful stories about God using ordinary individuals to make a difference in people's lives aroused something deep within me.

Reading this book left my heart with feelings of restlessness. As the weeks went by, I began to realize that God was calling me to a task, that there was something I must do. Although I didn't have a clue as to what it was, the feeling got progressively stronger and would not go away.

As weeks turned into months, it became evident that God was leading me to be a volunteer in prison ministry. Everywhere I turned there were stories about prisons or prisoners. Newspaper articles, television programs and magazine features bombarded my mind with the same message. But why? Where? How? *It must be a mistake. This can't be.* I became concerned and quite frankly, a bit frightened. I wanted no part of this. I didn't want to do it.

The Lord hounded me relentlessly, and I knew I had to pursue it, if for no other reason than to prove to myself that I had misunderstood the call. But the directive was loud and clear. *Go into the prisons.* His message touched every fiber of my being and was indelibly etched in my mind.

Step by step the Lord led me to the people necessary to clear the way for entry into the local prison. On Tuesday, January 4, 1985, along with a priest and several other men, I entered Lafourche Parish Detention Center for the first time. Filled with both excitement and anxiety, we met with thirty-five prisoners and shared the word of God. This continued for one hour each Tuesday night for seven years.

I went, but I didn't go easy. I resisted and fought all the way, always searching for an excuse or a way out. But none came. It was meant to be. A total of thirteen months elapsed between the initial call and that first fateful night. Little did I know of the huge impact these visits would have on my life, and in reality, they would prove to be a time of preparation for a much larger task in prison ministry.

Although these weekly visits followed no organized method or program, there was strong evidence of God working in our lives. Some prisoners wrote poems and essays giving thanks for their experience.

Difficulties getting into the Detention Center and personal struggles in my own life caused the visits to cease. Reflecting on those seven years and testimonies given by various inmates revealed that this endeavor had not been in vain. Hearts were touched and lives were steered in new directions. It had been worthwhile.

A one-year hiatus from this ministry left my heart empty. I felt a compelling need to become actively involved in prison work again. Coincidentally, John Musser, an attorney from New Orleans, called to recruit me as a volunteer for Kairos, a national prison ministry being brought for the first time to Louisiana State Penitentiary at Angola. Although John was a total stranger and I knew little about Kairos, I immediately said yes. After asking John how he came across my name and telephone number, his reply was, "I really don't know." Tears filled my eyes and rolled down my cheeks. Once again I realized it was meant to be. I had to return to prison.

The weekend began on a Thursday evening in March 1993 and ended on Sunday night with a closing ceremony. Forty-two prisoners were exposed to a highly structured but spirit-filled program. Talks, discussions, singing and prayer created the dynamics for a powerful, life-changing experience. It was amazing to witness the gradual transformation occurring in these hardened men. Hearts were softened, walls torn down and tears shed as they accepted Christ into their lives. It was awesome.

The closing ceremony afforded each prisoner the opportunity to share what he had received from the weekend.

Kairos has an excellent follow-up program to support the men in sustaining what they received on the weekend and to nurture their spiritual growth. Three years later, the growth continues. Has it made a difference in the prisoners and the prison environment? I believe it has. One security officer at Angola said, "We're glad you all came. It really makes a difference in their lives, a lasting difference." Imagine, this coming from a guard at Louisiana State Penitentiary, once known as the bloodiest prison in the South. With God's help, people can and do make a difference.

Working with prisoners may not be an endearing ministry to some. After all, most are criminals and social outcasts, and they deserve what they get. Right? They are also human beings and children of God. They are still someone's father, brother, son and friend. It is possible to love the sinner without loving or condoning the sin. Many prisoners have never been loved or have been abandoned by their families. Some will be released one day and perhaps move into your neighborhood. Wouldn't it be comforting to know that they have experienced a true change of heart and want to live a decent, productive life?

Prison ministry is extremely rewarding but very demanding. It requires an enormous amount of time and travel. That's the difficult part. But deep in my heart, I know that's where I must be and what I must do. It is God's will for me.

Curt Boudreaux

A Hug in Prison

*What love we've given, we'll have forever;
what love we failed to give will be lost for all
eternity.*

Leo Buscaglia

Two years before his death, I had the privilege of
accompanying Rabbi Shlomo Carlebach to a prison in
upstate New York. This time he had actually been invited
by the Jewish chaplain, who asked that he perform a
Chanukah concert for the Jewish inmates there. There
weren't many, not even a *minyan* (quorum needed for
prayer services), only about eight. There was no payment
involved, but Shlomo accepted the invitation without a
moment's hesitation. It was a shlep; three hours each way.
"No problem," said Shlomo cheerfully.

The concert was a huge success, and Shlomo made the
event into a real Chanukah celebration, but that was only
the beginning. When the Chanukah *chagiga* (party) was
over, Shlomo turned to the chaplain and said, "Please, I
would like to visit with the rest of the inmates here. Could
you get permission?"

Shlomo went into every cell, where he hugged, kissed and talked with each inmate. Then he went into the dining room, recreation room, kitchen, and every possible nook and cranny of the prison he was allowed. He wasn't satisfied until he had ferreted out every prisoner, making certain that no one had been overlooked. Finally, he was ready to leave, and we were walking down the hall when a big, burly, black inmate with a scarred, pitted face started running after us. "Rabbi, Rabbi," he shouted. "Please wait."

We stopped immediately and Shlomo turned to beam at him. "Yes, my holy friend?" he inquired sweetly. The man began to shift in embarrassment, almost as if he regretted his impulsive act, and then, finally gathering courage, blurted out, "I just loved that hug you gave me before! Would you mind giving me another one?" Shlomo gave him the most radiant smile in the world, and then tenderly enfolded him in his arms. They stood clasped together for a long time.

Finally, the inmate broke away and heaved the deepest sigh in the world. "Oh, Rabbi," he said. "No one, no one ever hugged me like that before." And then tears began to stream down his face.

"You know, Rabbi," he sobbed in remorse, "if only someone would have hugged me like that ten years ago, I surely wouldn't be here in this prison today."

Yitta Mandelbaum
Submitted by Dov Peretz Elkins

A Sunday at San Quentin

*The Apostles Paul and Peter and the Prophet
Jeremiah all went to prison because they knew
God. I came to prison to know God.*

Rico Johnson

I volunteered to assist members of my church in providing a service for inmates at San Quentin who could not
attend the regular Sunday service in the prison chapel.
These inmates were hospital patients unable to leave the
hospital area because they were HIV-positive. They were
confined to the hospital and nearby exercise yard. Little
did I know this ministry would have a profound impact
on my life.

Not even the beauty of the morning could suppress the
anxiety and fear I felt as I approached the parking lot near
the main entrance. I wasn't sure what to expect. A few
minutes later, my partner arrived, and we proceeded into
the main courtyard of the prison.

The prison chapel is the first building inside. We
stopped there to sign the visitors' log, then proceeded to
the hospital. On our way I noticed a large man in prison

denims with tattoos around his neck and up and down his arms. He approached my partner and gave him a big hug. After the greeting, he turned to me and said in a rather intimidating voice, "Who are you?"

The anxiety I felt earlier was nothing compared to this. In a kind of nervous, high-pitched voice, I responded, "I'm Mike."

My partner explained that I was with him, and we came to do the church service in the hospital. Then the inmate said, "Come here!" and he gave me a big hug. When we left, I asked my partner, "Who's he?"

"Big D," my partner replied. "He's the choir director for the chapel."

I thought *Wow. What a way to be greeted to San Quentin.*

As we proceeded toward the main cell blocks and through a large exercise yard to the hospital, a large group of inmates waited to enter the dining hall. As we passed, the noise and confusion overwhelmed me. My fear increased.

As we walked into the cell blocks, I was hit with a strong, unfamiliar, foul odor. The lighting was a subdued yellow and the surroundings depressing. At the end of the hallway a large metal door led into the hospital. My partner knocked and showed his ID through the window to the officer inside. When the door opened another officer escorted us to the exercise yard. After two more locked doors, we were in the "yard" outside of the hospital.

The yard has no grass or flowers. It's simply a slab of cement surrounded by high cyclone fences. At the end of the yard adjoining the building is a gun-walk above the yard where a prison officer paces back and forth with a rifle, watching the activities of the inmates. At one end of the yard is a makeshift handball court where several inmates played. On the side of the yard next to the cyclone fence are several stainless steel picnic tables.

Several inmates gathered there playing dominos and cards. Numerous other inmates were walking from one end of the yard to the other, then turning around and walking back to get exercise and relieve stress.

As we entered the yard, several inmates greeted us. Two of them ran to retrieve the garbage can on which we set up the altar. It consisted of a small box containing a cross, two candles, a small bottle with nonalcoholic wine and a container of wafers for Communion. We placed a white linen cloth below the box and inserted the candles and were ready to begin our service.

Seven inmates joined us in the nondenominational service. We read the Gospel and asked the inmates to respond how they felt about the reading. The inmates talked about the Scriptures and discussed how the Gospel related to them. The interpretations that evolved were incredibly moving and gave tremendous meaning to the readings.

The participants asked for prayers for their loved ones. Some asked for guidance and understanding. Others asked for improved relationships with fellow prisoners and prison officials. Then we prayed together for each other.

I noticed the depression that engulfed one of the inmates. I could see fear deep in his dark eyes. He seemed lost. He was very thin. He looked as though he hadn't shaved in days. His teeth were badly decayed and his hair was unkempt. I sensed that he was very ill.

When it came time for the "hug of peace," I approached the depressed inmate, hugged him and said, "Peace be with you." I sensed he was far away.

When it came time to serve Communion, I watched a small miracle unfold. I dipped the wafer representing the body of Christ into the nonalcoholic wine that represented the blood of Christ. As I placed my hand on his shoulder and tried to look into his dark, fearful eyes, I said, "This is the body and blood of our Lord Jesus Christ. Take in remembrance that he died for our sins."

As I placed the wafer on his tongue, his eyes lifted to mine, and I saw a faint smile begin to appear. A sense of calm came over him, and he seemed at peace with himself.

After the benediction, we dismantled the altar and the officers let us out through the gate. I looked back for the inmate who seemed so lost. I saw him walking across the yard with a coffee cup in his hand and a smile on his face. He seemed as though he was at peace.

I can't find the words to explain the feeling I had as I left San Quentin that day. All I know is that the anxiety and fear I had when I arrived were gone, and I too felt at peace. This whole experience was not about me going to San Quentin to "give" to someone else. It was about me going to San Quentin to "share" the spirit of God with others. That which I gave was returned to me one-hundredfold. When the peace calmed that inmate, I too lost all the fear about being there. All that mattered was the spirit of God that we shared together.

Mike Robinson

You have to expect things of yourself before you can do them.

Michael Jordan

Prayer for the Perpetrator

Dear God,

I recognize the evil of my behavior.
I ask forgiveness for the pain I've caused someone else.
Forgive me, God, and cleanse my heart.
Most of all, dear Lord, please send your angels to release me from
*   any yearnings to do again as I have done.*
May God cast out this evil from within me.
May I be returned somehow, through your grace, dear God, to the
*   ways of goodness.*
Please bless and protect those who have been victims of my
*   perpetration.*
May my life be somehow lifted up that I might be redeemed and
*   receive from you the chance to live the rest of my life on the path*
*   of good, through the grace of God and in service to humanity*
*   forever and forever.*
Amen.

Marianne Williamson

One Cup at a Time

Those that truly find God in the turmoil of prison's insanity are those that are likely to succeed.

Daniel Murphy

Nothing seems to bring people together like Christmas. The fact that I was now in prison made no difference. It didn't start that way at first.

The guards had placed a Christmas tree—roots and all—in each unit. The idea was for the men to make the decorations to go on it out of whatever they could find. Creativity was to be our only limit, with the winning unit awarded soda and popcorn.

The tree sat in the corner for a whole week. It seemed to be a symbol of the stripped dignity we all felt, being incarcerated at this time of year. Remarks were made by the inmates passing by as to what the staff could do with their tree. I, too, fell victim of the overall gloom that seemed to match the gray-colored snow clouds outside my window. My longing for home and hearth made my spirits sink to an all-time low. I thought of the chain of events that put me here. I was feeling so depressed that I couldn't even muster up contempt for those responsible for sending me to prison. All the blame seemed to come back to one person—me.

I walked out into the open space of the unit and sat down on a chair to watch the others pass by—going nowhere. I sat away from some of the men who were seated at the other end of a long line of chairs. Straight ahead was the tree, its branches brittle from neglect. Pine needles lying on the floor told of its need for water and even I, foul mood and all, could not deny a tree a drink of water. I went to my cell, got my cup, filled it in the sink and walked back to the tree. I was almost afraid to move a branch for fear of it cracking. Its need for water was worse than I thought. After several trips of carrying water, one cup at a time, a lifer by the name of Buck came forward with a bigger cup full of water.

All the water in the world ain't gonna help these roots, I thought. Just then a young man named Shorty handed another cup of water to me. Several dozen trips for water were needed before the roots showed evidence of being saturated. Shorty poured in another six or seven cups, filling the bottom of the tin tub that held the tree.

"Just in case it wants a drink of water later," he said.

As we stood around like medical interns who had just saved our first patient, it was Shorty who said what we were all thinking.

"It looks kinda naked, doesn't it?"

"I guess I could dig up somethin' ta put on it," Buck grumbled.

"I'll make the rounds and see who can help," said Shorty, taking off in a different direction than Buck.

I retreated to my cell with old memories of grade school running through my head, when glue and paper were crafted into wondrous masterpieces that Mom displayed with pride. My eyes shifted to a roll of toilet paper I had stashed away in a corner. Then I went on a hunt for a bottle of white glue that I had long since forgotten. After dumping my worldly belongings from the footlocker, I finally found the glue wedged next to some letters from my ex-lawyer. I like to take those letters out now and then. They were always good for a laugh—rereading the worthless promises of freeing me soon after a speedy retrial. To say the words were not worth the paper they were written on was truer than I ever imagined.

The letter-paper was printed with big gold stripes that ran down each left-hand border. A spark of creativity connected some two remaining brain cells of mine that had been dormant for far too long. I mixed the white glue with warm water until I had a thin milky soup. Then I took the toilet paper and unrolled a handful. By dipping it into the mixture, I could squeeze it out and roll long skinny sticks. I bent them in the shape of candy canes and laid them on our heater to dry and harden. With childlike glee, I took my lawyer's letters and with a pair of rounded kiddie scissors, I trimmed off the gold edging from every page. *My lawyer's letters are finally good for something,* I thought, as the radiator baked my creations into the shape of candy canes. I took the gold strip of paper and twisted a gold stripe down one of the drying sticks. *A fine job,* I thought, *even if I do say so myself.* They looked good enough to eat—all twenty-four of them.

As I stepped out into the unit, I was surprised to see a crowd of people around the Christmas tree. Buck was coordinating the trimming with all the tact of the cruise director on the *Titanic*. Handmade paper chains and ornaments were being hung everywhere. Someone had taken cotton batting out of three pillows and had balled it up to make a snowman.

Someone else had shredded the tinfoil potato chip bags into long strips and were hanging them as tinsel. I was not disappointed in the least when my candy canes got lost amongst the other wonderful items. The tree looked beautiful after a few hours.

We were all standing back to admire our work when Shorty came out of his cell carrying something. In his hand he had an angel. He'd covered a plastic bottle with the white silk lining he had cut out of his bathrobe, giving the angel a robe of her own. The head was made from a tennis ball and covered with hair he cut from his own head. He had cut the face from a magazine and glued it onto the angel's head. The wings were made of real pigeon feathers that he must have collected from the yard. Our angel looked a little weird, but it was the thought that counted.

Buck pulled up a chair for Shorty to stand on, and he proudly placed his angel on top of the tree. Shorty turned to all of us with a smile that was accented by his clumps of missing hair, asking, "How's that?"

"It looks right purdy," said Buck, and everyone agreed.

Our unit won first prize, and we enjoyed the soda and popcorn. Our tree was planted in the yard for everyone to enjoy, with hopes it would survive the winter. It did. The following summer was a hot one. A drought was killing everything, everything but the little Christmas tree, which somehow stayed watered all summer. Men carried water to it, one cup at a time.

Steven Dodrill
Submitted by Kimberly Raymer

Reprinted by permission of Charles Carkhuff.

Etched in my Mind

*Success is a state of mind. If you want success,
start thinking of yourself as a success.*

Dr. Joyce Brothers

It was one of life's short-notice opportunities. A schedule
change created an opening for me to speak for Operation
Starting Line. I was delighted to receive the call that they
needed me in Texas.

Operation Starting Line is a combined effort of more
than a dozen prominent Christian ministries, including the
Billy Graham Evangelistic Association, Prison Fellowship
Ministries and Promise Keepers. The goal of this evangelistic, discipleship and post-release program is to touch every
prisoner in the United States within a five-year period.

The events in Texas consisted of five teams who visited
thirteen prisons. I was part of a team of five, which
included an ex-prisoner—me. My job was to tell my story
of transformation from a life filled with poverty, despair
and drug addiction into a successful businessman.

My mother raised three children on a meager,
monthly welfare check while my father served time in a

maximum-security prison. Our house was filled with rats, mice and roaches. My environment led me to a life of crime in a struggle to survive. I recounted how Jesus transformed me from a Class X felon into a success.

On Friday we did two shows at a minimum-security prison. The next day, we went to a maximum-security facility. While we were setting up in the yard, the chaplain told us that if a riot broke out we were to go to the brick wall and put our backs against it and let the riot police do their jobs.

The unit was filled with boys, eleven to nineteen years old, who were serving thirty- to forty-year sentences. During the show, someone started a fire in the kitchen. When we returned two days later, we heard that many guards had quit because it was so dangerous.

We went to "the hole" (the administrative segregation unit) to speak to the guys in their cells. There I met a heavily tattooed seventeen-year-old "gang-banger" serving forty "ag" years. That meant he had an aggravated sentence and had to serve about thirty years before he could see the parole board.

In the hole, I sat on the floor and read the Bible with a sixteen-year-old gang-banger serving a ten-year sentence. When I asked him why he joined a gang, he looked at me like I was crazy and said, "Everyone I know is in a gang." I looked into his sad eyes and realized that only God could heal the hurts in this young man's heart. The incredible waste of a valuable life overwhelmed me. I asked him if he would like to accept Jesus into his heart. He eagerly responded, "Yes," and we prayed together. It was one of the most moving moments I had ever experienced.

On April 9, my team asked me to do "the close." Afterward, I told them that it was my birthday and there was nothing else that I'd rather be doing. Then I thanked them and began to walk away. As I turned my head toward the crowd, I was humbled to see the inmates, who were on their feet, blessing me with a standing ovation. The men were touched by my simple, heartfelt compassion. I realized that my job was simply to tell them my story and let the Lord take care of the rest.

A young man named Steve, came up to me after the show and showed me the scars on his hands where rats had bitten him as a child. He had previously accepted the Lord, but struggled with his daily walk. My heart was breaking for him.

As I reflect on these inspiring events, I think of the inmates' hearts that were touched by the hope that my life represents. Twenty-three years ago, I really was a seventeen-year-old convicted Class X felon. Moments before I cried out for the Lord's help, I was lying in my bunk, thinking about killing a prison guard.

Now the pain of yesterday is wiped away. I am happily married, live in a new house and drive a fine car. My life is blessed and radically transformed. Steadfast hope is a driving force that will keep prisoners seeking the face of God, giving him time to answer their prayers and implement his will in their lives.

At those events, Jesus touched many lives—including mine. My heart will forever see the faces of those inmates light up when I explained where I have been and where the Lord continues to take me. Their faces are etched in my mind forever.

Brian Brookheart

4

ON FORGIVENESS

Forgiveness is not the misguided act of condoning irresponsible, hurtful behavior. Nor is it a superficial turning of the other cheek that leaves us feeling victimized and martyred. Rather it is the finishing of old business that allows us to experience the present, free of contamination from the past.

Joan Borysenko, Ph.D.
Fire in the Soul

God Works in Mysterious Ways

I looked across the room and my heart froze! There, standing among the other inmates lined up against the wall, was a younger version of my recently deceased father. It was so uncanny that my husband, Andy, who was standing next to me, leaned down and said, "Do you see that guy across the room? He looks so much like your dad, it's creepy."

Outwardly, I'm sure I looked calm and composed, but inside I was shaking. *Get ahold of yourself,* I reasoned. *It's probably just a trick of the lights. Maybe Dad's been on your subconscious mind; after all, it hasn't been that long since his death.*

My childhood left much to be desired. My father and I had a talk years before his death during which we both agreed, he was not the father either of us would have liked. He had even given me the gift of an apology. Yet somehow, I still had the feeling that there had been no closure before his death.

How do I get myself into these fixes? Here I was committing to bring a weekend retreat into this prison with my husband and twenty-five other volunteers. *Get a grip,* I kept telling myself. Finally, I decided just to avoid the man all weekend. *I can do that; it's a big room, lots of people. No problem! What's the worst that can happen? I'm here now. Just keep plenty of space between you, and you'll be fine.*

I was snapped out of my mental argument when I heard my name called. "The outside leader of table six, Mary Rachelski. First candidate sitting to her left, Richard." I managed to weave my way to the table, trying not to make eye contact with him. I reasoned, *If I don't look at him, he can't see me.*

"Hello, my name is Richard." I turned to look into the watery gray-blue eyes of the younger version of my father.

This man not only looked like my father, but he sounded like him, same mannerisms, same way of combing his hair, same big words used out of context like my father. He even wore the same after-shave. God has a cruel sense of humor, doesn't he? Or does he? This man was like my father in almost every way, except that instead of making me feel stupid when I said something, he acted like I was the most brilliant woman on the planet! He validated everything I said and did. He laughed at my jokes. He got my snacks. He held my chair, and most of all, he never once made me feel shamed. Now, after the initial shock, I could see that he wasn't exactly like my father, but I had to admit that the similarities were uncanny.

One of the most important and beautiful exercises of the weekend is the foot washing. We reenact the foot washing before the Last Supper in the Bible. It's an immensely powerful experience, because everyone is totally connected emotionally. You may see a white man washing a black man's feet or a man washing a woman's feet. Everyone humbles himself or herself.

I had just taken the place of someone who had been kneeling on the floor washing the feet of others, when I looked up to see the next person to sit down. You guessed it; it was Richard. Except this time it wasn't Richard, it was my father. I started to cry. I was truly washing my father's feet with my tears. This was my chance to tell him I love him; I forgive him; and to go in peace. When I looked up again he was crying too, but he also had such a look of pure peace on his face. Then just as quickly, it was Richard again.

I couldn't wait to tell Andy what had happened on the way home. I wasn't sure if I was losing my mind. That night I couldn't sleep, so I wrote Richard a long letter, telling him all about my childhood and just what had happened that evening, and why it probably seemed to him that I must have been acting strangely that weekend. Only then was I able to sleep.

The next morning I received clearance from the chaplain to give Richard the letter, and to my surprise he had spent several hours writing me a letter. He asked that I wait until I returned home to read it. This is in part what it said:

> Dear Mary,
>
> I almost didn't go through with the foot-washing exercise. You see, I didn't feel worthy. So before sitting down, I asked God for a sign to show me that he could forgive me for all the terrible things I've done in my life, many of which I've shared with you in this letter. I've only told one other person in this world my secrets. When I looked down into your face, you were crying. I thought that was my sign, and then I saw your face change, to that of Christ's.
>
> The Peace of the Lord be with you,
> Richard

Mary Rachelski

If You Will Welcome Me

Life consists of choices. We can choose forgiveness, and to see the divinity in each person. This choice gives us a fulfilling life.

George Castillo

Once there was a man whose time had come to be released from prison in Pennsylvania. He had written to his wife, whom he had sinned against, and he had written to his children. He said, "I'm getting paroled next week. I've been in here almost eight years. I know you don't want me to come home, but maybe you would have some love left in your heart. I'm going to be on the 10:12 A.M. bus. I'll be passing by the house. And if you will welcome me, put a yellow sheet or yellow ribbons outside. Then I'll know that you'll receive me. If not, I'll just pass on by, and go away and try to get a job somewhere. And you can all forget about me, because I know how ashamed you must be of me having been in prison."

So the bus started down the road. Soon after, it stopped at a university and took on a group of students. They soon talked to the man and found out what was happening.

The young people became very interested in his story. They kept waiting for the bus to turn that special corner so they could see the house where he once lived. Would there be yellow sheets or ribbons to welcome him home? Or would the trees be bare?

When they turned that corner and started down that road, they could see a half mile away, nothing but yellow— yellow sheets in the trees, yellow sheets and ribbons all over the house. When the bus stopped, the man hurried off and fell into the arms of his wife and children to the wild applause of the students.

Billy Graham

Resentment or grudges do no harm to the person against whom you hold these feelings but every day and every night of your life, they are eating at you.

Norman Vincent Peale
Positive Thinking Every Day

Celebrating Forgiveness

One of the most lasting pleasures you can experience is the feeling that comes over you when you genuinely forgive an enemy— whether he knows it or not.

O. A. Battista

A seventeen-year-old murderer—hands cuffed, tears streaking his ashen face and a noose draped around his neck—was granted clemency seconds before he was to be hanged.

The man who spared his life? The murder victim's father.

Under Iran's Islamic legal system, whether the convicted boy would die was up to the relatives of his victim. After the boy's family and many of the public hanging's four thousand spectators pleaded with the victim's father, he told authorities to spare Morteza Amini Moqaddam's life.

The teen's family, overcome with joy, said they would never forget the act of mercy by the father, Ali Mohebbi.

"Ever since his son died I have been praying for him. I will never forget as long as I live how he gave me my son's life back," said Moqaddam's mother, who did not give her first name.

Moqaddam returned to prison in the ambulance that had been waiting to take his body to the morgue. He is expected to be resentenced soon.

Moqaddam was convicted of fatally stabbing twenty-two-year-old Hadi Mohebbi on December 13, 1999, after a quarrel about smoking in public. He was to be hanged from a crane fixed atop a truck thirty feet from the electronics shop where he committed the crime.

A dozen of Moqaddam's relatives, including his parents and grandmother, gathered in front of the shop before dawn, holding open copies of Islam's holy book, the Koran, and chanting, "Islam demands forgiveness. Forgive him for the sake of the Koran."

A crowd watched over by hundreds of antiriot police began to build in the working-class neighborhood. The street was closed to traffic.

Shortly after sunrise, a judicial official brought Moqaddam, dressed in a blue sweatshirt and sweatpants, out of the police car where he had been waiting. The official read out the death sentence and fixed a thick rope around Moqaddam's neck. The teenager's face went pale and he started weeping.

His family began screaming and turned to the crowd around them.

"Please help us," they pleaded. "He's only seventeen years old. Please ask for forgiveness with us."

Hundreds of people joined Moqaddam's family. About a dozen others shouted against clemency: "He should be killed," they yelled. "Otherwise he will kill again."

Mohebbi's father then spoke to judicial officials, saying he had forgiven Moqaddam.

The crowd rejoiced at the news, clapping, crying and shouting, "Allahu Akbar!" or "God is great!" Some lifted

Mohebbi's father on their shoulders, exclaiming, "Long live Mohebbi!" Even police officers joined the celebration.

Sunday evening, authorities brought the teen to Mohebbi's home for a meeting with both families. State-run Iranian television ran footage of Moqaddam repeatedly thanking Ali Mohebbi and kissing his hand and face.

"I really appreciate the father of Hadi, whom I owe until the last moment of my life," Moqaddam said.

Ali Mohebbi said he decided to forgive Moqaddam because "I just considered the honor of Islam.

"If I forgave him, maybe millions of people who would watch the news would learn about forgiveness—and that is the message of Islam," he said.

"When I saw his hands cuffed behind him and the noose around his neck and everyone was waiting for my order, I thought that first of all if this boy is dead, it will not bring back my son."

Afshin Valinejad
Submitted by Laura Lagana

Strangers Behind Glass

You never find yourself until you face the truth.

Pearl Bailey

Columbia County Jail. I entered the visiting room, found a seat near the wall and picked up the telephone that would connect me with my visitor on the other side of a three-quarter-inch Plexiglas security shield. The Plexiglas was clouded with age and the wear of too many harsh cleanings. The stools both my visitor and I sat on were made of round, bare metal and bolted to the concrete floor. In bright orange coveralls that were too small, I attempted to gain some sort of comfortable position as I looked through the glass.

"How is she going den, Kenny?" the old man said, his hands shaking as he held the telephone.

"Aw, it's okay. How are you feeling?" I asked.

"Oh, good as can be expected, I guess," he answered. I noticed his hands—they are nothing but skin-covered bones—not the big, powerful hands of the farmer, rancher and garbage collector he had been in days past. He seemed smaller somehow. His hair was gray, his eyes were bloodshot from the medication he was forced to take; even his voice seemed to tremble.

"Did you have to wait long before they let you in?" I asked.

"Naw, yust had a cup of coffee an' the guard let me in," he tells me in his English/Norwegian mixture that I knew so well.

"I got something to show you now, Kenny," he says as he takes an old metal box from a paper sack. Carefully he opens the box. I can see the box is antique, hand-painted metal. Proudly, shaking, he picks out a gold-plated railroad watch with a long, gold chain.

"Bet you never seen one like dis one before," he tells me as he tries to untangle the chain from the rest of the remaining treasures in his box with his free hand. Finally, he just lays the phone down and with shaky hands he separates the contents of the box.

"Yup, they just don't make 'em like dis anymore. Look at dis one too," he continues as he digs out several old wristwatches, some old gold rings and several dozen old coins. He shows each one to me proudly. They are his private treasures—he has found every one of them in the garbage over the last twenty-five years. Each item has its own little story of how he found it, when and where, and how lucky he was to have always looked into the garbage.

"Yep, one never knows what he will find, ya know," he says. I'm sad—I watch the face of this dying stranger—my father. Then I lie to him.

"Well, I think you are looking better these days."

"Oh, maybe some days it's better than others, you know," he says, trying to make light of what we both know.

"They tell me dat you might be leaving from the prison in the morning, Kenny, so I yust thought maybe I better get down an' see ya before ya go. So, you listen to me now, Kenny, yust in case something happens before you get out of dat prison. You listen good now, Kenny. If something happens, I want you to go see your sister, Sandra—she knows. It's about the house an' stuff, ya know. I already took care of everything an' Sandra knows what to do. I don't think I'll be able to get all the way down to dat prison to see you, so it's better we talk now," he says with his hands shaking and tears in his eyes.

My insides are turning to mush. I don't want to hear what he has to say, don't want to admit what we both know is the awful truth. He knows that death is just around the corner. We both know and can feel that this will be the last time we will ever see each other. A dying father, speaking his final words to his only son; two fractured hearts attempting to communicate; two grown men who love each other dearly attempting to face their final good-bye. He fingers those treasures before him, behind that scratched and clouded glass; each of us carefully avoiding direct eye contact. We are both afraid to face the other, years of guilt and shame, fear of tears and in denial of what is happening.

So many times I had seen the guilt in his eyes over the years; guilt he felt for the beatings I had suffered as a child from his once-big, powerful hands. So many times I wanted to tell him that it was okay; it was over; it wasn't his fault, but I never did. As time passed, my going to prison created guilt and shame on my part. Now we sit, strangers in guilt, father and son, bound by blood and love; strangers through violence and shame. I wanted to say, "Dad, I'm sorry your only son turned out to be the black sheep of the family, the only member of the family to ever go to prison. Sorry for the pain, shame and disappointment I've brought you." And I'm sure he would have liked to say he should never have beat me like he did when I was little, but we said nothing. We didn't even know how to say, "I'm sorry, and I love you."

"Your twenty minutes are up," the guard said.

"Well, guess I better be going," he said. "You take care of yourself now, Kenny."

"I'll be okay, Dad, don't worry about me," I said, watching his old and shaking hands gathering his treasures.

The tears come, I can hide them no longer. When he looks up, he too has tears streaming down both cheeks. Finally, we look directly at one another. In a trembling voice he says, "Good-bye, Kenny, you take care of yourself now."

"Bye Dad" is all I can manage to say.

I watch this old man through the clouded glass as he turns slowly and leaves the room in tears, in silence, speechless and in pain. I feel anger at myself for not taking the time to know this stranger that I love so much—this stranger I've always called Dad. Why didn't we go camping just once? Why didn't I try harder to lift the guilt he carried for so many years? Why have we never learned to talk to each other like the men we were, father and son? Now it's too late—time has run out; he is dying and all I can do is watch him walking away slowly, through this clouded glass, in tears.

"Good-bye, Kenny."

"Good-bye, Dad."

A father and son out of time.

My father died two months after I got to prison. I didn't get to go to his funeral, so I guess we were both right. It was the last time I would ever see him. Guilt and shame made us strangers to the very end. That clouded Plexiglas separating my father and me was, in fact, no more a barrier than the guilt and shame we had carried for so many years. The Plexiglas, however, I could touch with my hand; the shame I could only touch with my heart. Good-bye, Dad!

Ken "Duke" Monse'Broten

THE IN SIDE

Reprinted by permission of Matt Matteo.

I'm Sorry, Dad

Justice didn't do a thing to heal me. Forgiveness did.

Debbie Morris
Forgiving the Dead Man Walking

Dear Dad,

Even in my world of loneliness and misery, I cannot begin to imagine the pain and suffering you're being forced to deal with. My only wish is that I could be out there to look after you, as you have done so many times for me.

I know we had our differences in the past, and often-times tempers got the best of us. I guess when you're young, you think the whole world is at your fingertips and advice is the last thing I looked for. But still, you stood fast with patience and guidance. Now, when you need me most, the only comfort I can offer is in my prayers.

I'm sorry, Dad—I'm sorry for the shame and embarrassment my being here has caused to our family name. I'm sorry for the extra burden on you and Mom over the years. But most of all, I'm sorry we were so distant.

Was it only yesterday I was a kid growing up? Was it only yesterday you were spoon-feeding Melissa? That was almost fifteen years ago. Now I'm a dad. The only difference is, I'm trying to be a father from behind bars. It's not easy, Dad. I'm missing all the best years of their lives. Visits are always so short, and my letters can hardly fill the void in their lives. I miss them, Dad. And I miss you and Mom and the rest of the family. But no matter how rough things got for me these past couple of years, you never turned your back on me. That means so very much to me! I hope I can be half the father to Melissa and Stacy that I now realize you were to me.

I guess what I'm trying to say is, I love you. I suppose we never got around to saying that face-to-face.

Your son,
Dale

Dale Gaudet

The Gift of Forgiveness

Resolve to keep happy, and your joy shall form an invincible host against difficulty.

Helen Keller

Each time the barbed-wire fence closes behind me and I see the men sitting in a circle waiting for me, I begin to pray, "Please Lord, I want them to see you in me."

I'm often asked to speak to inmates about being the victim of crime. On March 23, 1995, my seventeen-year-old daughter, Nicole, opened the door of her father's house to a sixteen-year-old young man named LeVaughn whom she knew. LeVaughn came into the house and they began to argue over drugs.

LeVaughn picked up the butcher knife from the kitchen counter and stabbed Nicole to death. My only child lay dying on the floor of the living room, her eyes still open. The last sight she saw that day was the face of the young man who was killing her. This young man, whom I had never met in my life, came into my life that day and changed my life forever.

I buried my daughter, and one week later the district

attorney informed us he was asking for the death penalty for LeVaughn. He began telling us how he wanted to try the case, and then he proceeded to ask us if we believed in the death penalty. Everyone said, "yes," except for me. I said "no."

I don't believe in murder. Murder is murder, no matter how you look at it. It was no more right for me to take LeVaughn's life then it was for him to take Nicole's life. I did not need revenge.

I waited one year to be faced with the young man who had changed my life forever. He was hostile and angry during the trial. My greatest fear was that he would get the death penalty and that I would then have to fight to never allow that to happen. But God knew that wasn't how he wanted me to spend my time. LeVaughn was found guilty of second-degree murder and sentenced to thirty-eight years with no probation.

God had other plans for my life. LeVaughn still looked angry when he was sentenced two weeks later. Only now, he was sitting right next to me as I stood at the podium to address the court and the judge, but I was warned not to address LeVaughn. I was told I couldn't speak to this person who had changed my life forever, and he was sitting right next to me.

I began reading what I had written and then God spoke to my heart. I needed to talk to this young man. It might be my only opportunity. I turned and looked into his face. This was the face that my daughter saw as she lay dying on the living room floor just one year ago, and now I was looking into that same face. I told LeVaughn that I was not angry with him, but that I felt very hurt. I told him that I had compassion for him and that I hoped that he could somehow find a way to turn his life around.

And lastly, I told him that I would be praying for him. The face that was so full of anger was now looking at me in disbelief, and the anger was gone.

When I walked away from the courthouse that day, I knew that God had given both of us a gift. It was the gift of forgiveness. I was able to forgive the young man who murdered my daughter. Not because he asked me too, but because it was what God wanted for both of us. God was never going to be able to use me if I were angry. Forgiveness brings peace. And with that peace comes overwhelming joy, the joy of knowing that God will forgive me just as I have forgiven.

Two years ago, I became a Prison Fellowship volunteer. I also volunteer for the pre-release programs in several prisons in my area. I do a parenting program, personal development program and the victim's sensitivity program. I have also become a trained mediator, mediating minor offenses for the district attorney's office, and I'm currently working on a program to do mediations between victims and offenders of violent crimes. I believe in rehabilitation.

As I walk out of the prison I feel so much peace. I don't see myself as a victim. I see myself as someone who has had something happen in my life, and I chose to let God use it so that I might be of greater service to him. There is a sense of God's presence in prison. God is everywhere, even in prison. And to think I might never have known that—if I weren't able to forgive.

Kim Book
Submitted by Laura Lagana

Bringing Dignity

*Do not do unto your neighbor what you would
not have him do unto you; this is the whole Law
[The Torah]; the rest is commentary. Go learn it.*

Hillel
Elder Jewish Rabbi—First Century BCE

One day in 1970 I had my first encounter with violence.
An intruder had attacked my grandparents in their high-
rise Manhattan apartment. My grandfather was so badly
injured that it wasn't certain if he would live. My family
drove down from our home in upstate New York. The
two-hour trip was agonizing.

When we arrived, the apartment was still a mess: there
was blood splattered around the bedroom, on the walls
and carpet. What fury, what animal had produced this? It
looked like a scene from a nightmare. In the middle of the
chaos, my grandfather lay in his bed. I tiptoed into the
room and stood there looking at him.

His face was distorted. The attacker had hit him, stabbed
him, bit him. His eyes looked like those of a bullfrog, puffy
and slitted from where the attacker had tried to gouge

them out with his bare hands. The rest of my grandfather's body was covered with sheets and blankets, hiding the other spots where this man-turned-beast had tried to eat my grandpa alive and where he had stabbed him numerous times, venting his unknown rages.

"There are bites taken out of the soles of his feet," I remember hearing my mother say. In twenty-nine years I still have not gotten this picture out of my mind.

The attack, we were told, had happened at 5:30 in the morning. Upon hearing noises in the kitchen, my grandpa had arisen and seen a man frantically rummaging through the silverware drawers. It never dawned on him that this man was going to harm him or my grandmother, asleep in the bedroom.

"May I help you, sir?" my grandfather asked.

The man turned quickly, wielding a huge butcher knife. He approached my grandfather and said, "Gimme the white stuff." He led my grandfather to the bedroom, flicked on the lights and awakened my grandmother. The young man, who was apparently high on drugs, ordered her to get up and get him a towel. He had cut his hand open when he broke into their apartment. He approached my grandmother and held the knife to her delicate throat, a warning.

My grandfather knew at that moment that he was going to fight. *This man was going to kill us,* he thought, *two helpless old people in the early morning. But not without a battle,* my grandfather decided. He was going to fight and save my grandmother, even at the cost of his life. No one was going to harm his dear wife.

My grandmother handed the intruder a towel. As the stranger went into the bathroom to wash his profusely bleeding hand, he placed the knife on the side of the sink and turned his back to the door. My grandfather seized the moment. He lunged for the knife, grabbing it quickly, not realizing that as he did so he had grabbed it blade-end first. The knife sank into his hand, cutting and severing the tendons in his fingers. Still, he held on tight. He was fighting for life.

The intruder turned and grabbed my grandfather, a big man, throwing him onto the floor, and then picked up a floor lamp and smashed it over his head. My grandmother, a small woman, jumped onto the intruder's back, pulling his hair and kicking him, desperately trying to get him off of my grandfather. She broke her foot in the process.

My grandfather screamed at her to go get help. As she ran out of the apartment, the door slammed behind her and locked. She ran, crying and screaming for help, banging on the neighbors' doors in a panic.

Inside, my grandfather and the intruder fought for twenty minutes. As my grandfather felt himself slowly slipping into oblivion, drained, he uttered, "Oh . . . there they are. There are the police now." With that, the intruder fled. My grandfather crawled into the bathroom, painfully reached up to lock the door, and passed out.

The intruder was never caught. I remember going out onto Central Park West to trace the trail of blood left by this enraged, violent man. I followed it into the park as it dribbled away into a field of grass.

My grandfather miraculously survived, but my family was ripped apart. They were understandably full of hatred, full of vicious words and resentment. What happened to them almost scared me more than the senseless attack.

Part of me retreated because I was not feeling the rage that they were. Oh, I hated what this man had done. I hated seeing my grandfather, almost unrecognizable from the violent distortions evidenced on his face. I hated the rage and bitterness that was permeating my family. I hated all of it.

But I felt something different: I found myself wondering about the intruder. I wondered what had motivated him to do such a terrible thing. I thought, *How could one human being do this to another? What was wrong with him? Was he sick? He must be in a lot of pain and need help.*

Those were my thoughts, but I had no one to express them to. So I retreated inside myself, full of shame and guilt. Maybe there was something wrong with me because I didn't hate this man and wish harm on him.

I remember going to a meadow on top of a mountain in Woodstock, New York, where I always went to connect with God. I prayed to God to please fill me with whatever I was missing. I was so ashamed that I had compassion for this man who had harmed my family. But that hatred and desire for revenge never came.

To this day I often wonder whatever happened to that intruder. I really believe that we are all much more than the worst thing we have ever done. I really believe in the goodness of each and every one of us. I really believe in the power we have for change and recovery. Today when I go in the prisons and death rows I look every person in the eyes to connect and bring a moment of dignity to the human being, and I often wonder if I have ever looked in the eyes of the man who wreaked havoc on my family.

Jane Davis

5

ON KINDNESS

If there is any kindness I can show, or any good thing I can do to any fellow being, let me do it now, and not deter or neglect it, as I shall not pass this way again.

William Penn

The Gift of Friendship

Kindness is tenderness. Kindness is love, but perhaps greater than love. Kindness is good will. Kindness says, I want you to be happy.

Randolph Ray

My mother always told me, "If you have one true friend in your life, you are very lucky." As a teenager, I never really understood that expression because I thought I had lots of friends. It wasn't until much later I realized many of the people we call "friends" are really acquaintances who move in and out of our lives. As a mature woman, I must acknowledge I'm a very lucky person.

My best friend is also my roommate, companion, soulmate and husband of twenty-seven years. Tom is always there to lift my spirits, to support me through the big struggles as well as day-to-day problems and to overlook my weaknesses. Each day he tells me how wonderful I am, how nice I look and how much he loves me. I know I am not the easiest person to live with, but he's been putting up with me all these years, and I plan on basking in the warmth of his love and friendship for many years to come. However, I am writing this to acknowledge the existence of another wonderful friend. He, too, has become an important part of my life, and I am compelled to share our story.

Michael was a student in my third-grade class in 1973. He was bright, funny and full of life; he was one of my favorites that year. Tom and I took Michael and a couple of other boys camping that next summer because we enjoyed sharing our lives with children, and we had yet to have any of our own. Michael continued to be an excellent student and a leader, but once he left my school after the eighth grade, I didn't keep track of his progress as the years flew by.

In the summer of 1993, I received a letter from Michael that both shocked me and broke my heart. He was facing a prison conviction and was soon to receive sentencing. Would I write a letter to the judge on his behalf? Although I didn't know Michael as an adult, I did write a letter asking for compassion for this fine young man. As I mailed it, I wondered if I'd ever find out what happened.

A few months passed and Michael wrote again from a prison cell thanking me for my letter. It was a short note in which he informed me that his first chance for parole was the year 2002. I wrote Michael that same day expressing my concern for him. What could I do to help? Did he have the love and support of his family throughout this ordeal?

The letters began to flow on a regular basis. Yes, Michael was very grateful for the love and support of his family. He filled me in on the twenty years that had passed since he sat in my classroom. He had been a good student in high school and college and earned his MBA. He was a husband and father before this terrible tragedy. Now he lives in a six-foot-by-eight-foot cell and wonders what the future holds for him.

I was curious why Michael chose to write to me. I
didn't ask, but one day he revealed the reason. He had lost
his mother to cancer in the summer of 1976. He said that
he received a note of condolence from me, which his
father kept along with report cards. Michael would reread
it each time he needed something from the file. So, in
Michael's words, I had been giving him a hug about once
a year without even knowing it. That really started me
thinking about the importance of the little things we do
in life. To think that a note I don't even remember writing
would touch the life of a child so profoundly! For Michael
to call on me twenty years later still amazes me. How
many letters have I been too busy to write?

Each letter has brought us closer together. We tell each
other anything and everything. Sometimes I laugh and
sometimes I cry, but regardless, I can't wait for the next
letter to arrive. My heart overflows with love for him.

After five months of writing to Michael, I finally told my
husband what was happening, and that I had to go see
Michael. I had a real need to put a body and face with all
of the written words. So we made the four and a half-hour
trip, and I finally could substitute real hugs for all the
mental ones I had been sending. When we came out of the
prison that first time, I cried like a baby. I wanted so desperately to take him home with me and to make the
whole terrible situation go away. No one I know could
even begin to comprehend what it means to be an inmate
and to lose so many years of your life.

We visit Michael as often as we can. The smile on his
face makes the effort more than worthwhile. He assures
me that he is okay and he almost makes me believe it. The
visits are easier now and more relaxed, but the whole
process is heart-wrenching.

I once had a very naive point of view about inmates in
prison. They were all bad people as far as I was concerned.

But bad things happen to good people, and I know Michael is a wonderful, loving, sincere, good person. He made a terrible mistake, but he is paying for it dearly.

What truly amazes me about his character is his strength of fortitude and faith in God. He has learned to deal with his situation with prayer, patience and humor. He knows there is nothing he can do about his "time," so why complain? He also spreads that attitude to others. How lucky they are. How lucky I am.

Friends come in all shapes and sizes and under the most unusual of circumstances. We have to be ready to grasp each hand as it's extended to us or risk losing one of God's greatest blessings—a friend.

Diane Harshman

He who opens a school door, closes a prison.

Victor Hugo

You Never Know Who's Listening

Constant kindness can accomplish much. As the sun makes ice melt, kindness causes misunderstanding, mistrust and hostility to evaporate.

Albert Schweitzer

A friend of mine named Cynthia asked me if I would be interested in talking to a group of teenagers about the skills necessary for succeeding in "the real world." I love helping teenagers achieve success, so naturally I accepted.

As we were driving to the talk, Cynthia said there was something that she didn't tell me about this group of teenagers. My first thought was that there would be hundreds of them, and she was worried that I may be a little nervous, but that wasn't it at all.

Cynthia was taking me to speak to teenagers in prison. That's right, prison! She began preparing me for what I was about to face. She said that I would be speaking to some of the most dangerous, messed-up kids in Southern California. Some were in for theft, arson, battery and even murder. She said that I could tell who the murderers were, because they would be dressed in orange work clothes.

Cynthia was also kind enough to mention that these teenagers were only permitted one hour of recreation per week, and that I would be "stealing" their hour of free time. Didn't this just make me feel wonderful?

As the inmates came into the room, you could see that they really didn't want to be there, but I went there to do a job, and I wasn't going to be discouraged. Midway through my talk, some began heckling me while others simply weren't paying attention. I thought to myself, *What a waste of time.*

My talk was only twenty minutes, so they had forty minutes of free time to do what they wanted. Thank God! The only problem was that I wasn't permitted to leave until their full hour was up. So Cynthia and I remained in the room with the prisoners, anxiously watching the clock.

All of a sudden I noticed that one of the biggest, baddest-looking teenagers I have ever seen in my life was walking toward us. He was dressed in orange, about six-feet-five, weighing around 225. I became more and more nervous the closer he came.

Finally, he was no more than two feet away, and I thought to myself, *This guy is going to take a swing at me.* To my surprise he extended his hand and said, "Your talk was great. At first, I wasn't really paying attention because I was thinking of killing a prisoner named Joe tonight. But when you said, 'Wouldn't the world be a better place if we all simply just loved and cared for each other?'—it really hit me. All of a sudden, I began feeling love toward Joe, and I feel like I can do something with my life. I just wanted to say thank you, and I want you to know that I listened and appreciate that you came here tonight. No one cares about us. It means a lot to me that you took the time to come here. Do you think you could come back again?"

It was difficult for me to speak as I was choked with emotion. At that moment, I realized that I had done the right thing by speaking to the inmates. I was able to help at least one person, and that's all that mattered.

I reached out and hugged him with one of the tightest grips I've ever applied. As we hugged, I whispered to him, "God bless you."

Surprisingly, he replied, "No, sir, God bless you for coming here. You saved two lives tonight—Joe's and mine!"

James Malinchak

Reprinted by permission of Charles Carkhuff.

Chicken Soup

A kind and compassionate act is often its own reward.

William J. Bennett

I was dead tired. At the moment, I felt like I was only one small step this side of being dead. I was in Dallas presenting a two-day seminar and had spent this, the first day, frantically running between the seminar room and the toilet in the hotel bathroom. Now, I was sluggishly dragging my body up to my room, only half-aware that I had another day to go. I let myself fall onto the bed. It was only one of two times in my life that I felt simply too ill to take care of myself. I lay half asleep, dreaming of things like aspirin, chicken soup and a friendly face to make sure I survived this thing—whatever it was.

In the back of my mind, I remembered my seven o'clock dinner date with Carl. He had been an inmate at the Federal Correctional Institution in Bastrop, Texas, where both my husband Allen and I had worked as psychologists a few years before. I'll never forget his first appearance in my group in June 1990. He was at least six-feet-two-inches

tall and looked liked he had been dragged from a dilapi-
dated corner of Haight-Ashbury in the late 1960s. He had
a shaggy, ill-kept, grayish beard that reached toward his
abdomen and a wiry, gray ponytail almost the same length
that hung down his back. We called him "Bulldozer"
because of his quick-talking, unrelenting and aggressive
style. This turned out to be an unexpected asset for psychology programs—Carl was responsible for at least half of
the men at Bastrop enrolling in our groups.

Now, over seven years later, Carl looked more like an
army lieutenant than a hippie, and was operating a small
successful business in Dallas. He was content and doing
well, and we often jokingly referred to him as "our sure
success case." Whenever Allen or I went to Dallas, we
always made a point to meet with Carl. After his release,
and our leaving the Bureau of Prisons, we had begun a
friendship that was starting to take hold.

At about six o'clock the telephone rang. It was Carl.

"What's up?" he said in his typically brash voice.

"Can't go," I said. "Really sick."

I had learned to keep my word count to a minimum
with Carl. He always seemed on the run with things to do
and people to see.

"Oh! Yeah! Okay. Well, I'll see you later!"

Carl hung up the phone abruptly. *Well, that was that,* I
thought. Carl will never be mistaken for Mr. Rogers and
his friendly neighborhood.

I lay there in the dark. My hopes for a miraculous recovery were growing dimmer. The thought of performing
another day in front of a group was nervously etched in
my mind. The fact that this was a new client didn't help
my spirits rise.

A moment later the phone rang again. It was Allen, my
husband. "Hey, Carl called and said you're sick. He's on
his way over. Do you need anything?"

"Definitely a nurse—but some aspirin and something to eat would be nice," I said, hopefully.

Forty minutes later, Carl was at my door. I opened it with some hesitation. I looked wretched, and I was afraid he wouldn't recognize me, scream and possibly go running down the hall. But Carl didn't notice the greasy hair, the wrinkled clothes or the black circles. He just stood there with a broad, toothy smile and a bowl of chicken soup. He had driven over forty miles through congested Dallas traffic with chicken soup on his front seat, and had aggressively insisted that the hotel restaurant reheat it in their microwave to ensure that it was hot. Also stuffed under his arm was a bag with a six-pack of 7-Up, aspirin and a mango that he had taken from his own refrigerator before he left.

As I ate the soup, I lost all of my remaining reservations and concerns about Carl being a former inmate. Carl was no longer "Bulldozer." He was a gentleman. Suddenly, he became one of the people in my life that I had deeply admired and appreciated for that one special act of kindness.

As I tell this story to friends, they often remind me that this is a perfect example of the "Law of Reciprocity"—when you give to others, you receive in return. I believe in reciprocity, but I don't deserve the credit for Carl's kindness. This was not a simple example of kindness returned. Carl's kindness was bigger than that. The bowl of chicken soup reminded me that there is a light—one that is looking for a place to shine in every one of us. People who are incarcerated don't often have a place to shine that light. It simply goes unnoticed, and eventually dims and remains unused. Carl's light was burning brightly that night.

Also, in the moment that Carl handed me that first spoonful of chicken soup, I realized something deeply important—something that I had understood intellectually but hadn't felt in my heart. We are all in this thing called *life* together. Our work in prisons is not about one person—a psychologist, counselor, volunteer or chaplain—healing the prisoner's soul. Our work is about remembering the humanity in each other and not giving up.

I will never forget that moment when Carl stood at my door with his chicken soup for my soul. Carl taught me that kindness is not difficult—often, it is as simple as preparing a cup of chicken soup.

Each of us is in need of healing, and each of us is a healer. In a sense, we have all built our own prison, yet we hold the key to everyone's release.

Geraldine Nagy, Ph.D.

THE IN SIDE

Reprinted by permission of Matt Matteo.

Its Rightful Owner

A smile is the shortest distance between two people.

Victor Borge

I spent twenty years at Bastrop Federal Prison and didn't open up to the friendship around me until the last few years. My past crimes included assaults and escapes, and for the first fifteen years, I was known as one of the coldest, most hardened criminals in the system.

One morning while I was in the hallway, a prison psychologist, Dr. Geraldine Nagy, stepped out of her office and almost bumped into my 275 pounds of brutal hostility. As we made eye contact, a smile appeared on her face. "Good morning, David," she said, as she stuck out her hand. I was dumbstruck that she knew my name; I had never gone near her office.

I managed to say, "Good morning," as I shook her hand.

Dr. Nagy walked down the hall, then turned back and said, "Do you ever smile?"

"Yeah," I answered, "sometimes."

"Find somebody you feel comfortable with, and try it

today." She smiled, waved and walked away.

Dr. Nagy's moment of kindness toward me that day helped change my life. I took her advice and the smiles led to friendships—and ultimately to a pivotal, permanent change in me.

After twenty years in prison, I'm now free and successful. Practicing random acts of kindness and senseless acts of beauty helped hand my life back to its rightful owner—me.

David Smith
Submitted by Perry Arledge

Bittersweet Journey

We are here to help one another along life's journey.

William Bennett

My husband and I spent another wonderful afternoon visiting Michael. His positive energy and deep faith always renewed ours—he touched our hearts with joy. The shuttle-bus ride back to the main office was more upbeat than usual. Tom, my husband, even joked with the driver—comparing our ride to an "E ticket" at Disneyland. As our bodies jostled about with the bumps in the road, I recalled our first visit to the state prison eighteen months ago.

We went to see our friend, Michael, soon after he was transferred from another prison. We met him years before while volunteering on Christian retreat weekends. Witnessing the individual growth of these men and women became an incredible blessing to us. Michael was like a brother. He lovingly challenged us to be forthright and accountable while admitting his own struggles. He held no bitterness, forgave all and taught by example.

We knew little of the hardships involved in maintaining prison visits. It was a gift to share three hours with Michael, although it was a humbling experience. In the midst of beautiful mountains, this concrete fortress was a stark contrast. It was snowing sideways when we arrived.

At the main processing office, they told us that Tom's sweater wasn't allowed in because the color was too similar to the officers' uniforms. After Tom took the sweater back to the car, an officer told us we had just missed the first visit. We had to wait until after the count-time. We knew the Department of Corrections' rules and the need for total cooperation.

With paperwork properly completed and IDs in hand, we approached the next station. There an officer told us to remove our shoes and walk through the metal detector. Tom's belt set it off, which he promptly removed. We were finally cleared to sit and wait for the bus. Twenty minutes passed when a small bus pulled up to the door. Its seats were U-shaped, so we all sat facing each other.

Fortunately, our stop was first. We entered another processing office and turned in our paperwork. Tom made small talk, "I can't wait until we won't need prisons anymore."

The officer replied, "Not me. Job security!"

He stamped our hands and told us to wait for the cyclone gates to open. We entered and then waited for another gate. A cement path led down to the waiting room next to the visiting room. Someone gave us a number and said, "Wait until the inmate arrives." It was our first taste of what it must be like for hundreds of thousands of loved ones who go through these same motions week after week.

Through the window, I saw Michael and jumped to my feet. Tom reminded me of the rule to embrace only on entering and leaving—"So, be cool," he said. Mike looked great and wore the familiar blues and a big smile. He reassured us that he was fine and wanted to know how our family and his brothers in the ministry were. He paid in advance to have our picture taken together. Then he gave us the Polaroid shot, asking in return only our prayers for the ministry. We joined hands and prayed quietly amidst the noise of families and officers. The sudden announcement, "End all visits. Inmates line up against the wall," caught us off-guard.

Michael said, "I love you both and thanks so much for coming." Then he gave us each a hug. I felt a lump in my throat, and my eyes welled with tears. He was still smiling and waving as the officer led him through a door. I tried in vain to think of other distractions but still felt embarrassed, angry and frustrated.

Brave mothers with children stared blankly as they prepared to face another week of struggles most of us cannot imagine. Yet there I sat, traumatized by this sudden order to leave a loved one who had to endure a body search as payment for our visit. I thought to myself, *The system seems so cold and unnecessarily harsh.* Silently I thanked God for my freedom and the comfort of Tom's hand. It was a quiet, bittersweet, five-hour journey home.

We feel a social responsibility to encourage and support people to make the right choices in life, so they won't ever have to be incarcerated. Ninety-five percent of people in jail today will some day be set free. What can we do to encourage them to deal with their issues and make the positive changes so that when they're released, they'll be able to contribute to our society?

Normandie Fallon

A Few Kind Words

Wise sayings often fall on barren ground, but a kind word is never thrown away.

Arthur Helps

There I was on Christmas Day, in the lockdown unit. After having worked there as an officer for six years, I moved up the ladder and was eventually assigned to transporting prisoners, one of the better assignments available at the time. On Christmas there would be no transporting of prisoners. I was given the unenviable task of feeding the inmates who were locked down in the Special Management Unit.

The unit was always loud, and the aggressive inmates it housed were usually at their worst. Screaming, cursing and throwing food trays were the norm. On that particular Christmas Day I found myself preparing to serve the breakfast. Another officer worked along with me, assisting with the preparation of the trays and distributing the beverages. The meals were issued through an opening in the cell door, which we called the "chuck door." We knew that serving the meal would be a challenge because the inmates were upset and frustrated about being locked down on Christmas.

It seemed that as quickly as we passed the food trays through the slot, the inmates would throw them back at us through the chuck doors and onto the cell house floor. We endured many insults. I focused my thoughts on how I would soon be having Christmas dinner with my family. I decided not to take it personally and focused on doing the job.

One of the inmates was particularly nasty and vile that morning. His insults never ceased, continuing as we delivered the morning meal to each cell. Finally, as we were finishing up the detail and I began to secure his chuck door, I asked him to come to the opening in the door. When he did, I wished him a Merry Christmas and then secured the door.

Five months passed, and in late May I was approached in the yard by an inmate saying, "Ya know, you really messed me up." He repeated the message several times, and I asked him what he meant.

He asked if I remembered him. I replied, "No," and again asked what he was talking about. After refreshing my memory about the incident in the lockdown unit on Christmas morning, he told me, after his verbal assault, the last thing he expected to hear from me was a simple kind remark—"Merry Christmas."

He and I spent several minutes talking, and he shared how my words provided a wake-up call for him. He learned that not everyone was an enemy, and he recognized he was the one responsible for the choices he would make in his life.

I still ponder this exchange and remember what a few kind words can mean.

A. Douglas Rowley
Submitted by Mary Rachelski

Who Is the Tutor?
Who Is the Student?

One of the things I learned the hard way was that it doesn't pay to get discouraged. Keeping busy and making optimism a way of life can restore your faith in yourself.

Lucille Ball

I helped a fellow student learn to read when we were in fifth grade, and I've wanted to do it again ever since. Well, some thirty years later, through a long series of events that had to be more divine intervention than coincidental, I finally had my chance. I took a tutoring course through Literacy Volunteers of America. As I neared completion of the course, the local student/tutor coordinator called me and asked very hesitantly, "You wouldn't be interested in tutoring a prisoner down at the jail, would you?" I paused for a moment, thinking of my busy schedule and the requirement to meet away from the student's or tutor's home. By teaching a prisoner, I'd only need to consider one person's schedule—mine. The prisoner should be available virtually any time, and we'd have a perfect place to meet—the jail. So, I agreed to take on a convicted felon as a student.

Being a self-righteous, Miss Goody Two-shoes, I thought, *What a great opportunity. Not only will I have a chance to teach someone to read, but I can also set a good example for this guy and let him know someone cares about him. Maybe all this would make the difference in turning his life around. Wow!*

A few weeks later we met and began to work on his reading. At the end of the second lesson, he asked me if I would teach him to read his Bible. I had to stop myself from laughing out loud. I hadn't been to church except for weddings and funerals in more than twenty years. Furthermore, did he really think I was going to be suckered into believing he had had a jailhouse conversion? I told him, "I'm not sure that's something we could work on just yet. The Bible is a hard book to read with a lot of big words, but I'll see what I can do."

While I wasn't convinced he really wanted to know God's word, he had expressed an interest. I had been taught in the course to use material the student was interested in learning, so I located some Bible study material designed for adults at a low reading level. Near the end of each lesson, we'd turn to the Bible study material, and surprisingly, he would read it consistently with greater accuracy than the easier material we worked on earlier.

After many weeks of working together, occasionally I began to take him things such as brownies, cookies and pens. I always brought small amounts because I heard prisoners will use most anything for trading purposes. The next session after receiving these tokens, he would always thank me, tell me how much he had enjoyed them and who he had shared them with. *Shared?* I thought. I brought barely enough for one person, much less two or three. But, regardless of how little I brought, he told me how he had shared. This prisoner who had so little shared it all.

After we had completed several of the Bible studies, he asked me where I went to church. When I told him I hadn't attended since I was a teenager, he scolded me and told me I ought to go. Interestingly during that same time period, several people invited me to visit their church. As we studied the Bible lessons, we read one section on making choices, and we talked about the poor choices he made in his life that resulted in his incarceration. More was going on in my head than what he was saying. I had made choices, too, most of them good, but one in particular wasn't. I had consciously decided not to accept Christ as my Lord and Savior. I was a good person and could get by on that very well, thank you very much.

Fortunately, more and more "coincidences" happened over the next few months, and I began to attend church. Through working with this young man, in whom I could see Christ's qualities, I saw the need to rethink my previous decision. I feel very blessed to have had this prisoner touch my life and bring Christ into it. Who do you think was the tutor and who the student?

Nancy Waller

Impress Me!

There is no failure except in no longer trying. There is no defeat except from within, no really insurmountable barrier save our own inherent weakness of purpose.

Elbert Hubbard

Ron turned his chair so that it faced me, sat down, kicked it back on two legs and folded his arms over his chest. "Impress me!" he said with a sneer.

I shot back with, "I'm not here to impress you. If you think you can stick it out for the whole weekend, I guarantee you'll be impressed."

I was one of a group of twenty-five volunteers to bring a three-day retreat into a prison where Ron was an inmate. That was on a Friday afternoon in October 1993.

Lucky for me Ron appreciated a good challenge and took me at my word. He got into the atmosphere and camaraderie. Before long, everyone at the table was getting to know one another. As much as I tried not to fall back into my old habit of sarcasm, it just came naturally. He reminded me so much of my younger brother. By the end of the three days, he was crying in my arms.

The universal tactic for inmates whether showing contempt or camaraderie is sarcasm, banter and friendly put-downs, all of which Ron was the master. His sharp tongue wielded quick retaliation—his victim was often unaware of the attack until later. His winning smile could dazzle and distract even the most cautious potential victim.

As the weekend progressed a strange thing happened. Ron's sharp tongue started to relax. He took time with the slower inmates and showed incredible patience. He had natural leadership ability. It almost seemed as if he had been on this weekend before.

Ron's ability to coax even the most timid into opening up was amazing. He treated each person with respect, and his enthusiasm was infectious. Everyone began to look at Ron a little differently—including Ron. It was as if his conflict within had been replaced with an overwhelming eagerness to help others.

Although the team members and candidates represented a diverse group of religions, this Catholic-based program ends with a Mass. Ron made a point of sitting next to me during Mass. He peppered me with questions about the many changes in the Catholic Church during his twenty-two-year absence. He wanted me to help him brush up on his church etiquette, asking me questions like, "Do we still take communion on the tongue? Do you think God would mind if I go to communion without having gone to confession first?"

That macho facade was slipping away and suddenly he was a small child. He wanted to please God. That's why he was weeping in my arms. He told me that a drunken driver had killed his mother in a gruesome auto accident. The last time he set foot in church was to attend his mom's funeral. He was angry and he blamed God for her death. His mother was the mainstay of the family. After her death, they fell apart and went their separate ways.

He hadn't experienced unconditional love since then—until this three-day weekend.

That was the beginning of Ron's growth. He went through the Breaking Barriers program at the prison—a program designed to help people discover the obstacles to their growth. When it came time for Ron to share, he told us of his dream—of someday being reunited with his children. He painted such vivid pictures that we could almost smell his daughter's freshly washed hair as he brushed it in the sunlight. Every loving detail brought tears to our eyes.

Ron was using his natural leadership skills to help others. He had a newfound sense of pride in himself, and it showed. Everyone noticed the change in him, including his caseworker.

We tapped his thirst for knowledge when he eagerly agreed to help us establish a motivational library at the prison. He volunteered long hours setting up and cataloging all the donated books. He was like a kid at Christmas when a new shipment of material came in. He showed me how to type cards, bind books and gently break their binding so they could withstand years of use. We practically had to throw Ron out of the office at the end of the day so we could go home. He never thought of it as work, because he was doing it for others. One of his perks was getting first choice at the new material. Because of his insatiable appetite for knowledge, he became the perfect choice to run the library.

Ron was transferred to another camp to complete a required program to qualify for parole. Then Ron was a free man, but he actually became free on that Friday afternoon in October.

Mary Rachelski

Walking Tall in Toastmasters

Each and every step up begins with a step from below, and vice versa. But then the relative degrees of success and failure depend upon the motion and character of the person doing the stepping. . . . Walk good!

Marion Boykin

It was a cold winter night. A silent, freezing rain was falling, and I was alone. Only a few hours earlier, I had arrived at an Oklahoma prison with a life sentence. I felt hopeless, alone and lost to the world.

Pulling my denim coat collar tightly around my neck to ward off the cold, I walked past the bulletin board, looking for something—anything—to lessen my anguish. As others shuffled quietly through the hall, I stepped closer, squinting into the dim light. Then I felt someone close to me and quickly turned. A huge hulk was smiling at me.

It was one of those broad smiles that would grab anyone, and worth a million to me at that moment. The smile belonged to an old humped-over man in prison garb like mine. His eyes almost disappeared into the folds of his eyelids, sparkling in the faint light.

He said, "I'm Wilbur. C'mon with me to Toastmasters."

"What on Earth is that?" I asked.

Wilbur explained, "We help each other become better at public speaking."

At my first meeting of the New Dawn Club, I was greeted enthusiastically by the members. Wilbur introduced me as his friend and guest, and I soon felt like one of the group.

I noticed that my new friend was busy all evening. He put out ashtrays, greeted people at the door and served several pots of coffee. My cup was kept full during the entire meeting. As the meeting progressed, I noticed that Wilbur took no part. Oh, he listened attentively, and he always continued clapping a second or two after everyone else had stopped. In fact, I thought this was one guy who really enjoyed attending meetings.

Later, I discovered that Wilbur wasn't a member. As someone said, "Wilbur just shows up, he doesn't belong. He doesn't bother anyone." I knew then that Wilbur needed a friend more than I did.

Looking back, I guess ol' Wilbur was a little slow. Concerned with my own needs, I hadn't noticed it at first. Although Wilbur got along with everyone, he was considered a little strange.

As time went on, this group proved to be a lifesaver. Realizing that this could be a springboard to growth and betterment, I soon became a member and eventually served in leadership positions. All the time Wilbur was my mentor, my close friend and advisor. I counted on him, and he never let me down.

Once while I was president, a member was giving me a hard time over *Robert's Rules of Order*. The guy had me against the wall and wasn't letting up. At an opportune time in the midst of the argument, Wilbur jumped to his feet and said, "I move that all discussion cease!" Before Wilbur could sit down, and before anyone could come up with a "second," the matter was over. To this day, I'm still not sure whether it was done correctly.

Usually nobody took much notice of Wilbur. But he was well aware when his friend was in trouble, and he used *Robert's Rules* to an exactness that amazed everyone. He would wink at me, smiling that infectious smile of his, as he poured coffee for the man who had challenged me. He would even pat the guy on the back. That's just the way Wilbur was.

Still, Wilbur hadn't ever spoken at our meeting. One evening, when I was the host of the meeting, I looked over at Wilbur, and his smile told me he was ready.

I said, "Wilbur, in two minutes, tell us about your life on the streets." He arose with a flourish that astonished everyone. Holding his clasped hands together at his chest almost angelically, he said, "I would be most happy to speak on that subject." And he did so for a full two and a half minutes.

He told of his years on the oil fields, and how he had fallen from a high derrick and had to spend many months in the hospital, and of the steel plate he still carried in his skull. The crowd sat motionless, and at the end of the speech, it was as if a heavy load had been lifted from the entire group.

As I advanced through the group, I began to realize that this was more than a club—it was a challenge, a call to do better and reach out for full potential. I began to see it as a dare to envision something closer to perfection than we had known before. I saw it as a rare opportunity to help those who had been denied. I was astonished to realize I was changing, just as Wilbur was.

One evening we presented Wilbur with a completed

membership application and announced that the club had voted to pay his membership fee. Wilbur wasn't smiling then; instead, there was a tear in the corner of his eye. "Thank you," he said, and he continued pouring coffee. As soon as the attention was no longer focused on him, he glanced at me and winked.

Wilbur gave his first speech without my help. Looking back, though, I believe it was at this point we switched positions, and I became Wilbur's mentor.

We noticed that Wilbur didn't speak for a long time. He passed up several opportunities, and I began to wonder why. Then, one day Wilbur offered to speak in place of an absent member. He was well prepared, wearing his best prison clothes, sporting a new haircut and his warm smile.

His assignment was to understand the mood and feelings of the audience, to put those feelings into words and to inspire us. Wilbur did it all that night. Speaking about "Friendship and What It Means to Me," he spoke eloquently, carefully emphasizing important words—words he had not dared use before—and pronouncing each one perfectly. I was amazed at his growth.

He spoke of how much he appreciated the club's acceptance of him and the depth of the friendships he made. He spoke of leaving the prison soon, and of his pride in achieving his goals. Then he quietly sat down.

I realized that a gradual change had occurred in Wilbur. He moved slowly, and his step was not as sure as before. But he still retained his warm smile and that incredible sparkle in his eyes.

I saw the whole purpose of Toastmasters fulfilled in my friend Wilbur. He had developed self-esteem and was able to communicate with others confidently. I knew that Wilbur would make a positive contribution to his community. What more can an organization do?

Am I giving too much importance to this? I don't think

so. I've seen miracles in our prison group. I'm no longer surprised to see men come alive and work toward goals they once could not envision.

Not long after he left prison, we heard that Wilbur died. We weren't surprised to hear that his most prized possessions, his Toastmasters International certificates, were framed and sitting on the table by his bed when he died.

For years after, I still stopped by the bulletin board on my way to our meeting. I'd hesitate just long enough to turn and look behind me, expecting to see, even in the dim light, a huge hulk smiling back at me.

Rex Moore Jr.

The Gift of Music

Music washes away from the soul the dust of everyday life.

Red Auerbach

Ray could tell you how much he missed playing his guitar without speaking. Sometimes he would move his hands through the air as if he were playing his favorite blues scale. Even in prison, Ray always had a song in his head. One song in particular was very special to him. He had been writing it in his mind since the day he arrived at Gander Hill more than a decade before.

I went into the prison several times with my father who worked with Ray and others to start a group that helped inmates improve their communication and speaking skills. I was a college senior studying speech communications and had helped start a volunteer student group at school. Volunteering at the prison fit well with my interests.

Ray would come up to me, giving a slight nod, when he saw me come into the chapel for the meetings. He loved sharing his guitar stories. Ray described playing guitar as if it would make him a free man. Music was more than just creative metaphors for him; it was survival. He looked forward to playing again, the way a child counts the days until summer vacation.

In the spring of 1993, when the group was formally established at Gander Hill, the men were allowed a celebration and were able to invite one or two family members. The night of the celebration was like Christmas for those men. They huddled with their loved ones, whom they had not seen or touched in several months—some longer. Since his family lived in Texas, no one came to the celebration as Ray's guest, but he waited patiently for a very special visitor . . . me. As he rehearsed his song in his head, I walked into Gander Hill Prison that night with a guitar.

He prayerfully tuned that guitar as if he were putting the lost years of his life back into harmony. I have never heard a guitar tuned like that—before or since. It was the most beautiful tuning any musician could imagine. He looked at me over his shoulder and nodded thank you before bringing his song to life on the guitar. I watched Ray's fingers dance across the strings. They moved as if, through them, Ray was running free. And for those few short moments, he was.

Brandon Lagana

Reprinted by permission of Charles Carkhuff.

My Bag-Lady Friend and Me

The greatest healing therapy is friendship and love.

Hubert Humphrey

"Burn her! Burn the witch!" all the kids would tease.

This I remember clearly, thinking back to when I was in ninth grade. I had to take the subway across the city because I had been kicked out of the school close to my home. This was nothing new for me, since I found trouble easy. I can remember the nuns would always tell us to respect our elders, yet some of the same kids in our school were teasing this poor old bag lady.

Growing up, I was big for my age and a bully. I knew I could stop this abuse, if I wanted to, but no one would believe I'd do such a thing. To do so would show weakness. But something inside me kept tugging at my heart every time I saw the abuse of this poor soul—I had to do something.

I put my foot down and made some threats. You can bet, not one of those kids ever messed with that poor bag lady again. In fact, we became fast friends. At that time in my life, I was basically on my own—my dad was in prison and my mom was out most every night looking for "love."

There were no rules at home. I'd have a stolen car every day and pick up my new friend to keep her warm, or I'd see her in the subway and we'd hang out. Her name was Rose, and she had been a high school teacher until her husband and two sons died in a house fire. Something inside her snapped, and something inside me had already snapped.

Rose taught me so much! She was rich in wisdom, and I'll never forget her lessons. "Never judge a book by its cover," she would say.

Between sips of booze, she would tell me about God. How strange—this haunted woman still loved God and tried to share him with me, of all people.

We would sit for hours and talk about her favorite subjects—poetry and English literature, which she used to teach in school. There I was, hair greased back, a cigarette hanging from my mouth, wearing a black leather jacket, talking to a bag lady about God and poetry.

She said it was a release to write poetry when she was feeling alone. *Yeah, okay, sure, lady!* I thought.

Rose would only talk to me. Sometimes the police would come to my house and ask me to take her to the shelter. She was giving them trouble and wouldn't go when it was cold at night.

When I picked her up, she said I reminded her of her son and to make sure I did my homework. She handed me a poem and said, "I wrote this for you." When Rose got out of my stolen car, she said, "Get here early next time!"

That next time never came. I found her lying in the snow where we would meet—some said she waited all night. I was in the city jail for shoplifting some food for our supper. My beautiful bag-lady friend was dead—my little buddy, the only person in the world who broke through all the meanness.

Our next time together would never come, but that was the day I wrote my first poem, "My Bag-Lady Friend and Me."

We sat together on the orange line subway—
That beautiful woman, my bag lady friend and me.
I was on the run for some crime or another
But still we talked of poetry and things.
I said, "This line will take us to no where
And back again, it may take hours."
She said, "I've no where to sleep
And God knows it's cold out tonight."

Better go now. I've places to go and people to meet
Like two old paupers, we parted only to meet again—
She was my only friend, my beautiful bag lady
So rich in wisdom—everyone who did not know her
Laughed and threw stones—I cried.

That beautiful, mild woman
There's so many like her, my heart aches—
On finding her laying still in the snow, I cried—
She didn't labor to be beautiful, she was—
My bag-lady friend and me.

I sat down where we used to sit in the name of love.
I caught the last embers of the daylight die
And thought I could hear her say, "Stay for a while."
My beautiful bag-lady friend, "I've no where to sleep
And God knows it's cold out tonight." Let's talk.
I've missed you.

Jay Cocuzzo

Your Best Shot

*Show kindness toward another in their troubles,
and courage in your own.*

Princess Diana

The world is filled with beauty, joy and wonder, along with ugliness, hatred and violence. In my youth, I always believed that things were either black or white; people were either good or bad . . . that is, until I grew up.

When I became a nurse I saw many different sides of life, witnessed things that defied explanation and learned life isn't always fair. As I became a wife and mother, I discovered the gray zone that lies between the black and the white. I also discovered that there are no guarantees in life. You give it your best shot and hope that it's good enough. With this same attitude my husband and I approached parenthood. We both agreed that we would do our best to raise our two sons to be honest, law-abiding citizens.

I viewed both parenthood and my part-time position as medical-surgical nurse at one of our local hospitals as a journey into the unknown. Parenthood and nursing always yielded unexpected challenges and sometimes hidden rewards. I faced fear many times during my nursing career.

One December morning, I was "pulled" to the Protective Care Unit (PCU). When there was a staffing shortage in the hospital, the nurses would be pulled to that particular department that was in need. For some reason, I feared the PCU. I knew the unit was used to isolate patients suffering from infectious diseases, for reverse isolation to protect patients with compromised immune systems and to house inmates from the local prison who needed treatment.

For whatever reason, my fear remained strong. After morning report—the change-of-shift meeting where patient progress and updates are given—I prepared to care for my assigned patients. Suddenly I was forced to face my worst fear.

I was assigned to take care of a prison inmate—a convict. Suddenly I stopped breathing. I could hardly swallow, let alone speak, so I began to review my patients' charts. I reviewed the inmate's chart last, foolishly trying to postpone the inevitable. I decided to conceal my fear and meet my patients.

When I met the prisoner he wasn't at all what I expected. In my mind's eye I expected to see a large, disheveled, abusive character—instead, I saw a frightened, sickly child who desperately needed help. Jamie had appendicitis and was shackled to the bed, which was customary procedure for inmates. A correctional officer was posted at his bedside around the clock.

Jamie was amazingly frail and only several years older than our own two teenage sons. He tried to find a more comfortable position, despite the shackles. After I introduced myself and pulled up a chair, I began to explain his upcoming surgery to him. I quickly lost my fear, and I was determined to help alleviate his fears by preparing him for the operation.

Despite his obvious pain and discomfort, Jamie was eager to talk to me. As I took his vital signs and began washing his scarred face, he said with a grimace, "You know, you remind me so much of my mother. You could be her sister. You're so much like my dear, sweet mother. We had such good times. This time of year we'd bring in that huge Christmas tree, and then decorate it. Dad made sure to put that star on the top. Then we'd bake all kinds of cookies with icing and candies. Then, on Christmas morning there'd be hundreds of presents under the tree, and a big fire blazing in the stone fireplace. Oh, those were the good old days," he said.

When the vomiting returned, Jamie had to stop for a few minutes. After I cleaned him up, he continued to reminisce. "I sure miss those days. And I really miss my six brothers and sisters—three of each, you know."

"I'll bet you do miss those good times. At least you have wonderful memories," I replied. I didn't know what else to say. I couldn't stop wondering, *How does such a nice young man go so wrong? Just what happens to a person?* I never asked, because I didn't want to know—and I didn't need to know.

I read Jamie's chart and made a few notes. As I looked over his history and admission notes, I couldn't believe my eyes. Jamie had been abandoned at birth and had never known a mother or father. He spent his entire twenty-two years going in and out of foster homes and juvenile detention facilities—never knowing his natural parents—never knowing unconditional love.

This time, Jamie was serving real time in prison. I knew he had to have done something serious. I'm glad I didn't know what it was. I didn't want to think in terms of black or white, good or bad. I prayed that I could be a good enough mother to my sons so this wouldn't happen to them—but there are no guarantees.

The time for surgery approached. The orderly pushed

the gurney and accompanied me to Jamie's room. When the gurney and bed were aligned and the officer released Jamie's shackles, we helped him onto the gurney. As I pulled the sheet over him and placed the green paper cap on his head, Jamie looked at me through glassy eyes, a sign that the preoperative medication had taken effect. I felt the urgency to say something, so I took his hand in mine and said, "When you are released from prison, don't ever go back—make sure you stay out. Will you do that for me?"

He squeezed my hand and with a dry-mouthed, raspy voice responded, "Thanks, Mom . . . Thanks. I'll do my best."

I don't know if I made much of a difference that day, but I'd like to think so. Jamie, if you are reading this story, I pray to God that you are reading this from the "outside." I hope you gave it your best shot.

Laura Lagana

August 25

A diplomat is a man who always remembers a woman's birthday but never remembers her age.

Robert Frost

Before me stood a tall man, about sixty years old. He had a perfect crew cut, even though it was not the current style. He had bright blue eyes and wore a wide smile. He extended his right hand to mine, simultaneously reaching his left hand to my shoulder. It had been the warmest greeting I'd received in over three years. Then he handed me a business card that read "J. Richard Cook" on one side and "Happy Birthday to me—Remember August 25," on the other.

I had been startled by his humility because I already knew who he was. The inmates referred to him as their "guardian angel." He was the counselor to the Project Workers at the Plummer Community Corrections Center, a work-release facility.

Project Workers are inmates who have a prison sentence but are permitted to serve their sentence at the Center instead of a traditional prison facility. Project Workers are the cooks, maintenance people, groundskeepers, janitors, receptionists, switchboard operators and mail sorters. Project Workers who have their GEDs or their high school diplomas also serve as peer tutors to help others earn theirs. The Plummer Center Project Workers are also involved in community projects, from mowing lawns at churches to clearing snow from city streets and sidewalks.

The workers live in a converted house called the Mandatory Building. Their bunk beds are in a crowded bedroom instead of a cell. The building has a kitchen, dining room table, living room furniture and a TV. When the workers' loved ones comes to visit, they may hug them and eat the food prepared especially for them.

One worker shared, "As Dr. Cook and I sat and talked, I realized that he knew more about me than I know about myself. As we spoke about my crimes and my shortcomings, truth was the only option. There was no room for excuses or blaming others. He listened intently without judging or pitying me."

Dr. Cook would ask a worker, "Did you use your incarceration time wisely?" Then he'd briefly review their various responsibilities and how they were responsible to be on-call twenty-four hours a day. He'd say, "Your integrity must be beyond reproach. Nothing less will be tolerated."

After Dr. Cook met with a worker, he'd stand up, shake their hand and say, "Doctor, nice talking with you." He called people Doctor when he forgot their names. In spite of that, he still left the workers feeling more positive about themselves.

Dr. Cook escorted the workers to funerals, weddings, hospitals to visit a family member or to the train station when it was time to go home. I'd watch him take them through the prison gates. He could have used a state-owned car, but I knew he didn't, because the license plate read "AUG 25."

Dr. Richard Cook not only gave of his car, but he gave of himself. He was always there to guide the workers. He was a mentor, friend and critic—even if it hurt. He was a man with a colorful sense of humor. He had a basement full of treasures he stored for the inmates until their release and a phone bill lined with collect calls.

What did this man expect in return? Birthday cards, no matter whether they were from a store, homemade or from a computer. It didn't matter, but he only wanted one signature per card. He was even known to buy a box of cards and hand them out. He received cards from inmates released years before. Many had moved to other states and new successful lives. Dick Cook loved his birthday and everyone knew it.

On October 15, 1997, the Earth stood still. Our most beloved Dr. J. Richard Cook passed away in the place he loved—the Plummer Center's Mandatory Building—surrounded by those he loved and those who loved him.

The Mandatory Building was renamed The Cook Building and a tree now stands there in his honor. People still send birthday cards every year to our facility on August 25, even though they know Dr. Cook is no longer physically here. His spirit is alive and well. Thank you, Dr. Cook, and happy birthday.

Gail Valla

*A*nyone can stumble upon a treasure chest, but *it takes a thoughtful, patient and creative person to find the treasure inside.*

Brandon Lagana

Christmas Eve Behind Bars

Have you ever had an experience that stopped time? A time when you were focused on the moment and you felt a tingling burst of excitement, hope, love and joy?

Christmas Eve has always provided me with magical moments but they tend to merge, blending into a swirl of memories. These memories of family, love, music, and traditions, combine with a renewed faith and Christian promise. There is, however, one special Christmas Eve that will remain in my mind and heart forever.

A church representative asked us if our family would like to present a musical program for the military prison at Miramar Air Station in San Diego on Christmas Eve. We consented and suddenly the smallest decisions seemed crucially important. What to wear? What to play? We packed our songbooks and instruments, some balloons to twist and a Bible.

We arrived at the prison on December 24, and quietly unloaded our instruments. As we filed in, a lone uniformed officer greeted us. The main doors clanked shut behind us. The officer conducted a careful inspection of our musical instruments, looking inside the cases, including the music stands. He gave us a nod and told us to

walk through the metal detectors. After clearing the security door, we were led through a dimly-lit gymnasium
and then into a small classroom that served as the chapel.

Along the walls were large, built-in bookshelves that
contained assorted books and hymnals from varied religions. A modest electronic organ and a bench were nearby.
At the far end of the room was a six-foot table that we
staked out for the refreshments. We set up folding chairs in
gentle curves. The room was simple but serviceable.

A voice from the PA system announced that the musical program was about to begin. About seven to ten men,
each dressed in gray shirts and pants, filed in. They
appeared to be in their twenties and thirties—not much
older than my sons. We smiled and introduced ourselves
as they entered. There were no armed escorts, chains,
handcuffs, or numbers on their uniforms.

As they entered, we were busy blowing up red, white
and green balloons and twisting them together into creative shapes. We made festive balloon hats as a way to
loosen them up. The icebreaker worked—before long,
they were smiling and displaying their multicolored hats.

We passed out song sheets, introduced our family and
opened with the song, "O come All Ye Faithful." I fought
to suppress tears that threatened to cloud my eyes,
while I played the organ. The word "faithful" suddenly
touched me in an extraordinary way. The chaplain then
asked one of the men to offer an opening prayer, which
was a brief but moving expression of gratitude for the
evening celebration.

We sang religious carols and traditional Christmas
songs, along with Bible readings. Toward the end of the
evening we sang, "We Wish You a Merry Christmas."
Together we munched on cookies and chatted. With little
urging, the men ate all the cookies—they said they
weren't permitted to take food back to their cells.

It was quiet, polite conversation, but we knew these men were hurting. There was no outward evidence of their pain—we could just sense it. At the end of the evening we were grateful that at least *we* could leave.

On Christmas Eve, most of us eat a special dinner, wrap presents, and attend religious services. Over the years we've done all that, but that Christmas Eve in San Diego will always be different.

I believe that each of us lives in a prison of our own making. We can allow ourselves to become prisoners of our own hearts and emotions—restrained by the chains of unfulfilled goals and dreams that have dissolved. Four walls alone does not a prison make; it can be a place, a condition of life, or even a holding pattern—a place where we merely exist.

We held a party in prison. It was a celebration, a reaching out. Our lives touched; we exchanged hopes, spent time together, and made music. Our family never discussed that Christmas Eve behind bars. Perhaps it was too personal. We quietly processed it within our own souls. It was a compelling experience. Did we make a positive difference? Perhaps. Were the inmates somehow changed? Maybe. It really didn't matter because *we were!*

Nanci McGraw

6

ON LOVE

Every day I live I am more convinced that the waste of life lies in the love we have not given, the powers we have not used, the selfish prudence that will risk nothing and which, shirking pain, misses happiness as well.

Mary Cholmondeley

Love and Compassion in
Maximum Security

Compassion is the chief law of human existence.

Fyodor Dostoyevsky

My eighteen-year career in substance abuse treatment has been one of my many rewards. This work has provided me with the opportunity to see lives transformed as people overcome their addictions, convert apathy into empathy and develop a sense of love and compassion for others.

In the summer of 1992, James, one of the residents participating in a prison-based, substance-abuse treatment program, was diagnosed with cancer of the lymph nodes. As his condition worsened, he was transferred from the treatment unit to the prison infirmary to live his final days in seclusion. There he received the necessary medical services for his terminal condition. I went to the infirmary regularly to visit James, provide support and determine his needs. He was reluctant to ask for anything specific, but he was always appreciative of anything I gave him.

On many visits, I would deliver various soft drinks, coffee, chips or cookies donated by residents from our program.

At his request, James came escorted from the infirmary to the treatment unit and stayed an hour or so visiting with his friends in the program. The residents rallied around him and made every attempt to cheer him up—some told jokes, others gave him a poem or drawing, a cup of coffee or just a genuine smile. As he departed, they all lined up to give him a hug and offer words of encouragement. He always left the unit smiling and waving good-bye. As his condition worsened, James couldn't walk because of the swelling in his feet and legs, but he still visited his friends. I wondered which visit would be his final farewell.

In July, Darrell, who was a new graduate of our program, approached the staff and made an unusual request. He asked for permission to sit with James in the infirmary to provide support and ease the fear of dying alone in prison. Our warden granted this special permission so Darrell could be with James for several hours each day. Although James became weaker and death was knocking on his door, Darrell was there for him every day, giving him hope and inspiration to live.

Darrell spent his evenings and nights doing everything possible to make James more comfortable. James couldn't read or write any longer, so Darrell read to him, wrote letters and made phone calls on his behalf. He bathed and shaved him, fed him, wrapped his swollen feet with bandages and lifted him up when the nurse brought his medicine.

Near the end, James lost control of his bladder and bowel functions. Darrell was always there to patiently clean him up and change his bedclothes and sheets, to make it less humiliating for him. Darrell took special care of his patient, much like a loving father cares for a dying son.

Despite all efforts James died in his assigned bed in the maximum-security prison on September 16, 1992. He passed on with dignity, and on that day he was released from pain—and prison.

James left this world knowing that he had a true friend, who showered him with love and compassion despite their differences in race and religion. Love and compassion are alive and well, even in maximum security.

Bob Kennington

Reunited

For every obstacle there is a solution over, under, around or through.

Dan Zadra

John's wife became ill when he only had one year remaining on his sentence. Each night he prayed they'd be reunited one more time—to see her alive to tell her he was sorry, and that he loved her with all of his heart. Every day I'd see John out in the prison yard. I'd say, "How are you doing, my friend? How's your wife?"

"I'm fine, and Elaine is feeling much better. It looks like God is going to grant my prayer. I'll be able to see her after all."

"Listen, man, God is listening to you. Don't worry. She'll be there for you," I said.

"Do you think so, Doug?"

"John, I know so!"

John was released from prison on December 24. When he made it home that night, his wife, Elaine, had moved her bed by the window and was waiting patiently for his return. She greeted him with open arms, sincere kisses and tears streaming down her cheeks. The two of them spent that night in each other's arms as one—in life and in love. In the wee hours of the morning, they fell asleep—a peaceful sleep from which Elaine never awakened.

After the funeral, John wrote, "Doug, you were right. God did let me see her alive even though it was briefly. My prayers were answered."

Douglas Paul Blankenship
Submitted by Merry Disney

The Healing Touch

Young love is when you love someone because of what they do right. Mature love is when you love someone in spite of what they do wrong.

Mark Goulston

My first month of prison was in the spring of 1993. For a guy who never even had a speeding ticket, I was now facing a "life" sentence—my life became my worst nightmare.

I learned to cope in the solitude of my tiny cell. Each day, someone slid a food tray through the small hatch in the door. Eating became a necessity and far from enjoyable. Loneliness engulfed my world, and I felt like an alien from another planet.

I'll never forget my first visit. It was the first time in almost thirty days I'd be seeing my kids and family. I imagined feeling the small arms that would soon hug me and whisper, "Daddy, I love you!"

An officer led me down a dingy hallway to a small cubicle. There I waited, dressed in my red jumpsuit, staring out of a twelve-inch square piece of Plexiglas with tiny holes.

This was my first and most humiliating family reunion. It has replayed in my mind over and over again. I saw Melissa and Stacy racing up to the glass to see who could be the first to speak. My mom and dad were looking old, tired and fighting back tears of pain etched in their smiles. My mom is hard of hearing and too proud to wear a hearing aid. Over the noise of some two dozen families visiting in booths like mine, it was almost impossible to hear on either side. It was overwhelming.

I had remained strong throughout the trial, hiding my emotions from my kids. Now, looking at my entire world through smeared and scratched glass, I could no longer hold back the tears. I felt ashamed and lost. It was then that my eleven-year-old, Stacy, squeezed forward and placed the palm of her hand against the glass. Even with all the shouting and distractions, nothing could prevent me from reading my daughter's lips as she smiled and said, "I love you, Daddy! Everything will be okay!"

As I pressed my hand to the window, it was then that I felt the "healing touch." Before long, both girls had their hands pressed tightly against the window and if only for a moment, we were reunited. The feelings of shame and pity I felt only moments before were replaced with love, support and determination.

The "healing touch" renewed my faith in family, God and myself. *Together, we'll survive this ordeal,* I thought. There's an old saying, "God made tears to wash away the pain." We've cried a river of tears since that first visit and have grown closer as a family, although we're miles apart.

I believe there was a guardian angel sent to me that day. It took the simple innocence of a child to bring my life back into focus. It took coming to prison to show me how much I really lost.

Just the other day, I received a letter from my little girl. On the back page, drawn in pencil, was an outline of her hand followed by the words, "Daddy, I love you. . . . Everything will be okay."

I still have those drawings. In fact, over the years, I have recorded important events that have occurred in their lives as a reminder of how important they are to me. My kids are my lifeline to reality. Maybe one day, I'll send their drawings back or trace my own hand holding all the memories I missed out on over the years. Who knows . . . maybe one of those precious memories will even say, "This is the day my dad came home."

Dale Gaudet

How Do I Love Thee?

If you love your work, you'll never have to work a day in your life.

Thomas Edison

One day, a friend asked me how I fell in love with my husband. She said, "How could someone like you fall in love with someone in prison?"

My friend never even met Robert. This irritated me, until I realized that I used to think the same way about people who had criminal records.

About a month after I met Robert, I found out he was on parole. I learned this by accident and was shocked. Robert said he didn't want me to know for fear of what I'd think of him. But by this time, I knew he'd be my future husband, and it didn't matter—I loved him anyway.

Sure Robert made some mistakes, but after his last incarceration, something changed. At first I told everyone he was maturing. I believe that was a small part of it, but I've come to realize this change is more due to being able to release his anger at the world. Anger and pain caused him to turn to alcohol and drugs for the answers he couldn't find anywhere else. Robert changed most when he turned to God for help. He still feels some anger and pain, but God gives him the strength to get through it.

I fell in love with Robert's compassionate heart and his deep soul. I fell in love with a man who, despite a hard exterior, has eyes that show his true emotions. He's a man who has pulled himself up with the help of God.

While in prison, my husband wrote and told me he was grateful I never gave up on him. He was glad I saw something in him he couldn't see in himself. Through him I learned that not all people in prison are bad. In fact many are misunderstood, and the majority just need someone to have faith in them, to help them gain the strength to change direction.

I wrote a poem about my husband. Perhaps sharing it with you will help you, too.

> *My best friend and my lover;*
> *My companion through the journey of life.*
> *All these things you are to me*
> *Through good times and through strife.*
> *I look into your eyes*
> *And see all my dreams in there.*
> *My heart knows no boundaries;*
> *My soul knows no fear.*
>
> *God's placed you by my side*
> *And there you'll always stand;*
> *Shoulder to shoulder, eye to eye,*
> *Forever hand in hand.*
>
> *Most times I walk beside you.*
> *Oft' times I walk behind . . .*
> *To be able to watch over you*
> *When you have a troubled mind.*

My need for you is great.
My love for you is true.
My husband and my hero,
I give my life to you.

Cecilia Thomasson Baker

Serving Others While Serving Time

The only ones among you who will be really happy are those who have sought and found how to serve.

Albert Schweitzer

After being released from thirty hours in a holding cell without a bed, I was shown to my bunk. I was scared, angry and upset—mostly with myself. My designated spot was the top bunk (without a ladder), in a group of four double bunks. They were squeezed in a small alcove outside some cells. The prison was overcrowded with nearly a thousand prisoners in a facility meant to hold less than four hundred.

I arrived there about 1:30 in the morning and collapsed in exhaustion, despite the bright overhead lights.

At 6 A.M. we were awakened for breakfast, which consisted of a small box of cold cereal, milk and Kool-Aid. In the bunk below me was a stocky, bald man in his mid-thirties, who introduced himself as DeMo. It took me a while to get the rhythm of his speech. He not only spoke in street language, but he had a slight speech impediment.

DeMo asked me, "Wha fo dey gots an old man likes you up dere?"

"I guess it was the only bunk available," I answered.

"We sees bout dat," he said, and left me wondering what he had in mind as he walked purposefully down the stairs to the tier below. He came back a few minutes later, and informed me that one of the other prisoners in our little alcove was moving to another module that day, and I would be moving into a bottom bunk. Later, I found out most inmates had to wait several months before moving to a bottom bunk. DeMo also got me an extra pillow and blanket. He filled me in on the basic routine of our module, which contained about 120 prisoners on two levels. I thanked DeMo and asked if there was anything I could do for him. He assured me there wasn't.

Now, I have to confess I was somewhat suspicious of his kindness and hospitality. After all, this was just my third day in jail. He didn't seem a likely candidate to make any undesired advances, and I couldn't imagine what else he might want from a fifty-six-year-old man. My cynicism quickly abated as I began to understand that what DeMo most craved in his life was order in the midst of chaos. He made certain our little alcove was always clean and neat, no one stole anything and we got extra treats from time to time. This crack addict and dealer from the streets of Oakland was a superb manager of his environment.

As we became friends, I came to understand DeMo. Through his numerous experiences in prison, he learned that serving others was a satisfying way to serve time. I started looking for ways to contribute. I became a human spell-checker for the upper tier. When an inmate was writing a letter and needed a word spelled, I was there to shout it out.

When I was transferred to a federal institution, we had typewriters available. As an accurate and fast typist, my services were in high demand, so I found another way to serve. I became friendly with Jihad 2X, the Nation of Islam minister/inmate, who was a gifted, though not professionally trained, speaker. I shared some of my twenty-five-years of experience as a professional speaker with him.

Another friend, Luis, was intimidated by a literature course offered by the local community college. I encouraged him to overcome his insecurities about the English language. He in turn helped me learn some Spanish.

I did these things because they took me out of myself and out of my own difficult situation. They also empowered me. Although I'm serving time in prison, I can still encourage and support other human beings. There's nothing more spiritually rewarding and satisfying on this planet than loving and serving others.

Jerry Gillies

The one thing we have to offer in this life, of any real value, is our time to others.

Richard Ogren

"I understand prison overcrowding
has become quite a problem."

Reprinted by permission of Christian Snyder.

A Letter from Mother Teresa

The things a man has to have are hope and confidence in himself against odds, and sometimes he needs somebody, his pal or his mother or his wife or God, to give him that confidence.

Clark Gable

When I first came to prison in 1991, I was bitter and depressed. I thought I'd write to Mother Teresa in Calcutta, India. Frankly, I didn't expect a reply.

To my surprise about four weeks later, I received a letter postmarked from Calcutta. It was from Mother Teresa in her own handwriting.

I had told her how disappointed I was and how angry I was about almost everything. She told me to forgive those who had hurt me, for my own peace of mind. She also told me to forget my anger. It could only hurt me more than others. She urged me to look around in prison and try to help relieve the suffering of the others around me. I thought this was strange, but I shared her letters with other prisoners, and I was surprised to see big changes in their attitude and behavior.

Mother Teresa reminded me, too, that Jesus had suffered and died for me and for all mankind, including prisoners.

Later, she wrote, "Thank you for your sharing. It is beautiful to know that you allow my simple words, from so far away, to bring His healing love to your troubled heart. I encourage you to continue to help others around you who are hurting by spreading the fragrance of God's love through your compassion for them in their own trials."

In one of her earliest letters, Mother Teresa told me that every morning her congregation of nuns, the Missionaries of Charity, prays in their Motherhouse in Calcutta. Part of their daily morning prayer is, "Lord, help me to reach out today to anyone who may be hurting in any way. Let me listen to them and tell them of your love for them." It was amazing to me that when I shared this message with other prisoners, how much calm and tranquillity resulted.

One young man from New Jersey had been a Mafia hit man. He wept when Mother Teresa wrote to me to give him her message of love. I think it changed his life. What always amazed me was the simplicity of her message. Why hadn't we seen this before? It took a humble woman in India to remind us that peace and love begin with us. If we want peace and love in our lives, we must be willing to give peace and love to others. No wonder such words seem radical.

Just before she died in the fall of 1997, Mother Teresa wrote to encourage me to continue to promote Love Day, which I had begun, to honor her and her work, to be observed on October 7 every year. Nearly forty governors have written their support of Love Day, and she was very pleased that her message would be shared so widely throughout the world.

In her last letter, just weeks before she died, she asked me to remind anyone who would listen that the greatest disease in the world today was "poverty of the spirit." She urged me to tell others to "commit random acts of kindness and deliberate acts of love."

Mother Teresa's letters to me are for prisoners everywhere. They bring light in the dark and hope to the hopeless.

Lou Torok

The Life . . . of Death

I first met Larry a few years ago. Knowing the spiritual work I did in prisons, coupled with Larry's zest for things of the spirit, his parents suggested I meet him. Larry and I corresponded and he put me on his visitors' list.

I didn't really know what to expect the day I arrived to see him. What I knew, as I always know, was that a human being was going to come out and meet with me.

In Texas, all death row visits take place behind glass and wire mesh. Once a man goes to death row, he never again touches or hugs his loved ones. Not even on the day he is killed. Final good-byes are said behind glass, even to one's children and mother.

I sat on one side of the wire-ribboned glass, waiting for Larry to come out and sit on the other side. A young-looking, balding man with bushy eyebrows and intense eyes was led to his chair. He wore the prison whites of Texas and a gentle, beaming smile. My hands automatically went up on the glass, fingers spread wide as if giving an alien hug. His hands met mine on the other side. We smiled and nodded and took a deep breath acknowledging, in some unspoken way, where we were. Death row.

Larry had been sitting on Texas's death row for seventeen years. When he was a teenager, he was diagnosed as paranoid schizophrenic but was refused help from the state because he wasn't violent. One day he killed five people. Instead of receiving help, he was sentenced to death.

Over the years, I came to know Larry as an intelligent, caring, searching human being. Strange words to apply to one who carries the label "mass murderer." But even Larry searches for an answer as to why he really did what he did that fateful night and has spent years trying to meet with the victim's families to apologize and provide a space for them to heal. When I first met him, I had no idea what he was on death row for. While that is often the first question asked of me—"What did he do?"—it is often the last thing I come to know about the people behind bars.

In August 1999, Larry's time had come. He had his date with death: August 17, at 6 P.M. For Larry, that was all right; he was prepared to die.

Preparing for death is not like getting ready for a dance. It is an integrated challenge of the body, mind and soul. People living on death row live with death differently than anyone else. Larry prepared for years for this moment; in the final days and hours he combined fasting with prayer and focus.

Larry has often told me, "They can't kill me." It's one of the theosophical beliefs he holds; others have used that quotation to question his sanity. What he means is that his physical body can die, but his soul—his spirit—will go on. His belief in the hereafter is one of the gifts he cultivated, these last years, daily revolving around death. Facing death, whether it be as a result of a fatal illness or execution, has a way of strengthening one's life.

The final hour that Larry was allowed to spend with others was spent with those who were spiritually connected with him to help prepare for his moment of departure. While the noise of the prison visiting room echoed around us, we created a place of peace within a harsh, cold, deadly environment. Five of us sat in a semicircle on one side of the glass as Larry, adorned with wooden prayer beads, faced us. For an hour we meditated together. Virtually no words were spoken except a whispered "I love you"; heads nodded in solemn, gentle bows as we offered final good-byes.

The next time we would see Larry he would be strapped to a gurney with an IV needle in his arm. He would not look at us. His path, Sant Mat—a Sikh derivative—teaches him to be focused on where he is going and not to take any connection to this life with him.

But it was not to be. An hour later, as he was arriving at the Walls unit in downtown Huntsville, he was notified that he had received a stay. He had already sent all of his belongings for bequeathing. I was told that he looked out the window, silently, when told the news. Generally a stay is something to celebrate. In Larry's case it was bittersweet.

I received a call from a state-appointed psychologist. He wanted to know if I thought Larry was mentally competent. The competency law in Texas is simply defined: First, does the person understand the imminent nature of what he is facing—in other words, death—and second, does he understand why he is being executed?

It was a humbling moment for me. I was being brought face-to-face with telling the truth. Never did I ever imagine that telling the truth would contribute to the killing of a human being.

I knew Larry had given this man my name and number. I also knew he wanted me to speak the truth as I knew it.

"Did Larry ever speak to you about his burial arrangements?" I was asked.

"Yes," I answered and described what he desired to be done with his remains.

"Did Larry ever talk with you about bequeathing his property?"

"Yes," I replied and shared what Larry wanted done with his books, his poetry, his writings and his musical instruments.

"Is there anything, in all the time you've met with him, that you could share that might indicate that he is not competent?" I wept quietly, feeling the enormity of the questions and the answers. "I wish I could lie," I whispered.

Larry was executed on January 21, 2000 and declared dead at 6:16 P.M.; seven minutes after the first chemical entered his system. In the week prior to his death, Larry repeated words expressed over the years. "I did a terrible thing taking the lives of their loved ones. To say 'I'm sorry' seems so hollow. I wish I could tell you why things happened as they did, but it is all still very much a mystery to me. I hope they will be able to forgive me."

It's often abhorrent to many people to apply the word "human being" to those who have crossed certain human lines. One of the most valuable lessons I continue to learn from Larry—and others who live in prison and death row—is not only the depths to which man can fall, but also the spiritual heights to which man can rise and change and grow. This applies even to those who have murdered and raped.

All I know when I meet a human—whether inside the walls or out—is that I know nothing about him or her. I merely yearn to know my "neighbors"—their good inclinations as well as evil inclinations—so I can practice applying the gut-wrenching, humbling action of love.

Jane Davis

The Waiting Game

Don't wait. The time will never be just right.

Napoleon Hill

What's it like as a woman waiting on the outside for the man you love on the inside? That depends on your attitude. You can resist and be angry, or go with the flow and accept the constant change of rules and procedures.

David and I chose to look at it as a time to love each other in creative ways. We couldn't exchange gifts, but we could give of ourselves in imaginative, fun ways.

For example, on our first Christmas, we each wrote a story about where we would go and what we would do on our first real outing, with no restrictions or limitations on imagination. In my story, I picked David up on "Baby Cakes," a white-winged unicorn with glittery red hearts all over her. We flew to a pink castle nestled in the Alps, and that was just the start of our romantic adventure. We exchanged our stories and agreed to open them at a designated time on Christmas morning and feel the love. We created a fairy-tale world and shared adventures most people never experience in their lives.

Monday was our visiting day, and we spent eight hours playing and really talking. If no cards were available we played the game "Hammer, Paper, Scissors," laughing like children. Sometimes we only had a partial deck of cards, so we would make up new games. Do you have any idea how much fun you can have with a box of animal crackers? Your partner picks a cracker, and you guess what animal it is. Then you have to make the sound of that animal before you can eat the cracker. This all takes place in a room full of guards, inmates and visitors. To make it even more exciting, the winner of the games gets to make a win-win request of your partner— like, write a happy memory from your childhood and share it with your family. You always have until the next visiting day to fulfill your request. You can deny a request, but we never did.

We spent this sacred time of being totally with one another doing eye work: no words, no physical touching, just looking into each other's eyes and allowing the full presence of love. It made the guards nervous at first, because they were sure something weird was going on. In fact, the first time we did it, the guard came over to David after a few minutes, tapped him on the shoulder and escorted him out of the room. The guard told David they had been watching us and didn't understand what we were doing. We hadn't been touching or anything else they could see, and that made them nervous. David explained it was a simple exercise called an "Eye Dyad"— you are just present to the person in front of you and without words, you send them love. He returned, tickled that we had upset all the guards with our exercise. They finally agreed it was harmless and allowed us to have this small bit of personal, nontouching intimacy. After a while, they seemed to feel the presence of love, and it spread to other couples in the room.

We plan to keep "Sacred Mondays" as a special gift from our journey. Inner peace is wanting what you have. Our intention is to have a loving and peaceful relationship, regardless of what's going on around us. The last six months of David's incarceration were the hardest, because we found ourselves desperately wanting it to be over. When we chose to be at peace where we were, we were then able to release the struggle and slip back into peace.

On those Mondays, we experienced a new level of intimacy—one of the bittersweet gifts of incarceration—that we might never have discovered in other circumstances.

We plan to keep creative play as an important part of our lives and our relationship in the future. By the time you read this story, we will be together—married as man and woman. It is our turn to experience our fairy tales. "Baby Cakes" is ready to take us on a new journey. The Waiting Game is over.

Perry Arledge

Meet Me at the Bridge

The hardest thing in life to learn is which bridge to cross and which to burn.

David Russell

In the early years of our relationship I found it harder and harder to walk away from a visit. . . . I thought a "forever" loomed in front of us before we could live our lives together. The loneliness that engulfed me as I left each visit seemed to stretch so far out that it seemed impossible to tolerate!

My husband has an incredible sense of humor. He finds the positive where only negatives seem to exist. Together, we found a way to "deal with it," not to constantly talk about next year, or three years from now. We learned to just "make it" from one visit to another . . . and visits became known to each of us as "the bridge"! In our correspondence, in our conversation, we refer to "making it" from one "bridge" to another. Honestly, the image of a bridge was in my mind because of a book I and millions of others read, and then millions more flocked to see the movie: *The Bridges of Madison County*. A "bridge" symbolized for us a special place to meet, a secret only we were sharing.

And what about that bridge? How have two hours spent at a wide table where holding hands is honestly uncomfortable (sitting in the midst of other visitors and under the watchful eyes of employees) become so special? First of all, we acknowledge that span of time is ours, and we *talk*. I honestly doubt that many married couples in the free world spend two whole hours at a time in their week really communicating! Elijah knows that I am sentimental, a "romantic" by nature. He kisses the palms of my hand; he takes all the blue M&Ms out of the package for me because that is my favorite color, and he unceasingly expresses gratitude. Gratitude is an attitude; I believe that! Elijah says thanks for every snack, for every mile I travel to see him—and his "thank yous" are sincere. I have learned through the years how special it can be to be genuinely appreciated! In the midst of a crowd my wonderful husband is willing to blow me a kiss each week before he goes through a door and is out of my sight once again. It truly is the "little things" that count in life!

I truly do my best not to think about next month or next year, just the next bridge. I can recall how convinced I was that my husband would be paroled, but I don't get to vote. Setbacks have taught me to stop looking ahead and to appreciate what very little time we do have together.

Recently we tried something new that worked for us. I bought a paperback copy of *The Green Mile* for my husband, knowing that the movie would soon be released. He suggested that I buy a copy for me, too. We each read the book during the week and discussed it at our visits, and when I saw the movie, I was viewing for two. My "movie review" at our Sunday bridge was very real for my husband because we had just finished reading the book together.

Perhaps it sounds unrealistic to you, but when Elijah does come home, I want the bridge in our lives to continue. Every Sunday I want us to spend two whole uninterrupted hours talking to each other; I never want that level of communication to diminish in our marriage. I also believe that if we keep the bridge in our schedule, it will serve as a special reminder of where we came from: two people who met with glass separating them, who waited years for the first touch and the first kiss, who learned to appreciate every moment together. . . . For as long as we live one of us will look at the clock on Sunday afternoon and say, "Meet me at the bridge!"

Nancy Muhammad
Submitted by Thomas Ann Hines

A Mother's Comfort

The worst prison would be a closed heart.

Pope John Paul II

New to the Catholic Detention Ministry, I felt apprehensive as the chaplain and I walked into the prison module bringing our prayer service and communion to the Catholic inmates. My mind was full of questions . . . *just how will they be able relate to me, a chubby, middle-class, mature woman with nothing more in common but our love of God. Perhaps I may not be able to provide much of what they need.*

These were only some of my misgivings. Yet, after the service, as the men filed out of the room, the first part of the answer to my question was clear. While shaking their hands, each inmate smiled and thanked me for coming. It was quite obvious that they viewed the mere presence and touch of people from the world outside as a special gift.

When the line drew to an end, I noticed an extremely young man, with a baby face, beaming as he approached the door. His sweet face overwhelmed me, and the urge to throw my arms around him and give him a big hug was too strong to ignore. In spite of previous warnings against this type of closeness, and without thought, a big hug was exactly what he got. Shocked by my own action, I vowed to maintain better control in the future—but it did feel good.

The second part of my answer came, a few weeks later, in a letter to our chaplain from this same boy. Shortly after our visit that day, he had been transferred to a maximum-security facility in another area. These were some of the words he wrote:

> *I'm okay . . . just a little scared because this is my first time in prison. I'm locked down about twenty-two to twenty-three hours a day, but that's okay. Nothing will happen to me if I'm in my cell.*
>
> *Thank God!*
>
> *How is Mrs. Felicia doing? I hope I got her name right. She is really a nice lady. I remember the first time she came with you. At the end of the service, I was the last one to walk out, and she gave me a big hug. I wanted to cry in her arms, because I miss my mom a lot, and it felt so good.*

Without a doubt, working through this frightened young man and myself, God answered my questions completely. I was exactly where I needed to be. This work was a blessing. A blessing not only for the men, but for me as well. I vowed from that moment to trust my inner feelings when visiting these souls. Then I will most certainly know that they are getting what they need.

Felixa Miller

Through the Years
Standing by You

Not a day passes without me thinking of you. Through it all, the good and the bad, I have always stood by you. The dreams and plans I had for you even as a baby when I held you close to me.

I will always stand by you.

Words cannot describe the excitement your daddy and I felt each time you caught a pass and sailed into the end zone. The pain of shattered dreams.

I will stand by you.

When the drugs entered your life, your daddy and I were devastated, feeling that somehow we had surely failed you. Not knowing what to do or where to turn, the dreams and plans became just a distant memory of the past—turning loose of the dreams that would never be.

I will still stand by you.

Then came the prison years. I watched you age before your time. A young man of twenty-nine that looked forty. Your years of incarceration have been hard on the family, but through it all, we stood by you.

If I had my life to live over, I would still stand by you.
I will always love you,
Mom

Virginia Pool
Submitted by Thomas Ann Hines

7

OVERCOMING OBSTACLES

*I can choose to sit in perpetual sadness,
immobilized by the gravity of my loss, or
I can choose to rise from the pain and
treasure the most precious gift I have—
life itself.*

Walter Anderson

THE IN SIDE

Reprinted by permission of Matt Matteo.

Releasing the Prisoner Within

Bitterness imprisons life. Love and forgiveness release it.

Nigel Risner

Each month when I enter the doors of the Transition House, our local homeless shelter, I look up to God and say, "Here I am willing to do your work. I am grateful to be a volunteer and not a resident."

The evening was quiet and the shelter's guests were out in the yard as the volunteers arranged dinner. I noticed a quiet and distant young man sitting at the dinner table. I went up to him and introduced myself but was quickly ignored. I went back to the kitchen and continued to help prepare the food. After dinner the young man kept to himself. Once again I tried to start a conversation with little response. I asked his name, where he was from and how he found himself in a shelter. Finally he began to give me a little information, but he was not willing to share much. As it grew later, I finally broke through his resistance with my constant questions and friendly prying.

In an angry, controlled voice he said, "Look, lady, my name is Joe, and I'm here because I just got out of the pen. Is that enough?"

My response was, "I was just curious. What did you do to get yourself into prison?"

He looked at me with wild eyes, and replied, "I murdered a guy—all right?"

I took a deep breath and asked, "Who did you kill—and why? Since I'm about to spend a night with you in this shelter, I think it's only fair you let me know, don't you?"

He was young, about twenty-five years old, with blue eyes and blond hair—someone who desperately needed another chance. I could feel it and see it in his eyes.

Slowly he began to tell me his story. His best friend had been in a near-fatal motorcycle accident and was in critical condition at a local hospital. Two other bikers from a rival club found out about the accident and went to the injured friend's apartment and broke in with the intent to harm his girlfriend. They beat her, raped her and left her on the floor to die. When Joe found her barely alive, he took her to the hospital, and then went looking for the two guys. When he found them, a fight developed. During the fight, one of the men fell to the ground and sustained a fatal head injury. Joe was found guilty of manslaughter and sent to prison.

By the end of Joe's story, I was crying. My heart was filled with compassion for him. His eyes were filled with tears of sadness and shame. I held his hands across the table and said, "Thank you for telling me your story, Joe. I feel safe knowing you'll be sleeping here to protect me tonight. You're a brave man to defend your best friend's girlfriend. I'm so sorry it took so much of your life away."

As we both cried, Joe responded, "Thank you. For the first time in seven years, I feel accepted. I feel released. You'll never know what you've done for me." Then we hugged. I listened and accepted him as Joe, not as an ex-con.

We all need to be accepted as human beings, not as labels given to us by society. I felt privileged to be the one to help release Joe's "chains of guilt" that night to truly set him free from prison. It's in loving that miracles happen.

Judi Weisbart

Guilt not only doesn't decrease our negative behaviors, it guarantees their repetition.

Allen Nagy, Ph.D.

The Writing on the Wall

I know not whether Laws be right
Or whether Laws be wrong;
All that we know who live in gaol [jail]
Is that the wall is strong;
And that each day is like a year,
A year whose days are long.

Oscar Wilde

In bold black lettering, someone had scribbled "Johnny Has Full-Blown AIDS" in a vestibule in one of the dorms here at Sing Sing. After complaining for five days, I got off my butt. Taking a spray bottle of window cleaner, a paper towel and scouring pad, I tried to undo the damage done by an uncaring person with a black marker. I had visions of others seeing me scrubbing off the graffiti and felt a bit of fear over it.

I was sure the graffiti would never come off. As I aimed the cleaner and pulled the trigger, to my surprise, the cold and malicious message began to run like mascara on a rainy day. With two strokes of a paper towel, Johnny's name and HIV status were wiped clean. To my relief and shame, no one saw me.

Back in my living quarters, I questioned myself. Why did I wait five days to do something about the graffiti? I'm sure that everyone, including the superintendent who passed through that vestibule, must have seen it too. I thought, *Someone else will do something about this. It's not really my problem.*

I remembered the Kitty Genovese case from the '60s. She was repeatedly stabbed as her screams went unanswered in the early morning hours. Her assailant took over thirty minutes to murder her, while thirty-eight neighbors watched from their windows behind locked doors. Were all those people so detached from one another that all they could say was, "It's not my problem"? Would we let history repeat itself at Sing Sing? Would I allow another Kitty Genovese to happen here? Maybe not, because of the writing on the wall.

Most of us have a secret or thought that we don't care to share with the rest of the world. Someone robbed Johnny of that choice. Even if it's tough to keep secrets in prison, we can still have dignity and respect.

Who is Johnny? I don't know. As someone who teaches classes on HIV/AIDS awareness, I wanted to share with him the pain and shame of my procrastination. I hate that feeling.

Weeks later at an awards dinner, I spoke of the incident. Our superintendent and his staff were present, along with others who live in the building where the graffiti was written. The effect of my speech was more powerful than I expected. A man in a Con Edison uniform came up to me and said, "Doing the right thing means doing the right thing, no matter how long it takes you to do it." As a community, sometimes we let too many things slide by that are wrong, when all it may take is a little elbow grease to make the world a better place.

Radames Rios

An Attitude of Gratitude

*Gratitude unlocks the fullness of life. It turns
what we have into enough, and more. It turns
denial into acceptance, chaos to order, confusion to clarity. It can turn a meal into a feast
. . . a stranger into a friend. Gratitude makes
sense of our past, brings peace for today, and
creates a vision for tomorrow.*

Melody Beattie

Teaching optimism is my biggest challenge. As a life-
skills teacher in a juvenile detention center, my students
come to class with a wide assortment of attitudes. Some
view incarceration as a cleansing—a new beginning.
However, most are cynical, pessimistic and view the
whole world as their enemy. I've come to realize that
many of my students don't value their lives, don't have
goals, don't see realistic dreams and aren't aware of their
many strengths.

During several Oprah Winfrey TV shows in 1997 and
1998, she and her guests discussed the principle of gratitude. They stressed the concept, "If you focus on what

you have, you'll end up having more. If you focus on what you lack, you will never have enough."

Guest after guest, including children, related the changes that came into their lives just from the simple act of noticing the good they found in life and then expressing their gratitude. One woman fighting cancer coped better with her pain by writing about it in her journal. She and her husband focused on the good things in their lives.

On the show, author Sarah Ban Breathnach suggested that a good way to acknowledge gratitude is making a gratitude journal. From her I learned that within a few months, we become different after consciously giving thanks each day for the abundance we have in our lives. We set an ancient spiritual law in motion such that the more we have that we are grateful for, the more that will come our way. As we fill our journals with blessings, an inner shift in our reality occurs. As we focus on the abundance in our lives rather than on the lack of it, we design a wonderful new blueprint for our future. That's gratitude at work, which can transform our dreams into reality.

I experimented with this concept with my students. First, I showed them the Oprah tape on gratitude, and then we made gratitude folders. I said, "Doing this will change your perspective on life and help you be more positive."

You could see some facial expressions in the room showing their disagreement. One student yelled out, "There ain't nothing in here to be grateful for!"

I challenged each student to test the theory. Their assignment was to look for five new things each day that they were grateful for and write them in their journals. After five days, I asked them to share how their journal helped them. Here are a few of their comments.

"It makes me feel better after I'm done writing in it. I'm going to take it with me after class and write more."

"I think it's a very good idea, and it makes me realize

what I'm grateful for. It gives me something to look forward to and be happy about."

"Thinking about positive stuff keeps you happy."

"I like doing the book cause it gives me self-esteem."

"I like it a lot. It makes me focus on the good."

"I think the gratitude journals are a good idea. They make us realize things that we usually overlook. They make me feel better about myself because I am being more grateful. If you didn't continue the gratitude journals in class, I would continue writing in it anyway."

I've heard almost everything from, "We finally have something good to eat here" to "I'm getting healthy enough to run the whole time in gym" or "I'm losing the bags I had under my eyes when I came in here." One gratitude that is mentioned the most is, "I'm grateful for my family coming to visit me here."

In *Man's Search for Meaning*, author Viktor Frankl, a Holocaust survivor, states: "We who lived in the concentration camps can remember the men who walked through the huts comforting others, giving away their last piece of bread. They may have been few in number, but they offer sufficient proof that everything can be taken from a man but one thing: The last of his freedoms—to choose one's attitude in any given set of circumstances, to choose one's own way."

Teaching students optimism is still challenging, but using a gratitude journal helps us maintain an attitude of gratitude.

Judy Worthen

Memories

God gave us memory so that we might have roses in December.

J. M. Barrie

In 1971, I married a beautiful, tiny, long-haired lady named Sherrie. As a result of that marriage, my only daughter, Shirley Ann, was born. She soon became Cissy to me. She also became my best little buddy. When Cissy started to talk she called me Bom-bee. Every other father in the neighborhood was either Dad or Daddy—I had to be "Bom-bee." It didn't take Cissy long to figure out that a mournful-sounding Bom-bee was all it took to get her way with me or escape taking her nap. She ran as fast as her fat little legs would carry her to greet me when I entered the house after work. Those are good memories.

In 1973 my parole was violated for drinking, and as a result, I was returned to prison. Sherrie filed for a divorce, and I lost my little buddy. Many times over the following years, I prayed silently for my little girl. Sometimes in tears, late at night, alone in my cell, I could almost hear my little buddy saying a sad "Bom-bee." I asked God to protect her and that whomever her new stepfather was, he would be a kind and understanding person, and that someday I would be able to find her again. Those are painful memories.

As time passed, I was to survive three full-scale prison riots, see countless assaults, witness several murders and earn a college degree while in prison. I fought several fights as a professional boxer. I even fought a named heavyweight contender from the Seattle area. He beat me pretty badly, but he never knocked me off my feet. I guess I've always been kind of proud of that fact. Those are violent memories.

I was on a national television program called *48 Hours* as a spokesman for transitional release of inmates in Oregon. They sent a nationally known commentator to interview me.

After the television program aired, many people came to see me—mostly media types. They had only to call the associate superintendent and say they wanted to talk to me about being on *48 Hours* to be cleared for one visit. Most of the people who came were from the local media. They have a hurried, rumpled look about them, from making deadlines, no doubt.

One day as I returned from work, the cell-block officer told me that I had a visitor, a Mrs. Donald Honnen, who had seen me on television. So I washed up and went to the visiting room. I noticed her right away when I entered the visiting area; she was looking out of the window and had that nervous, hurried and rumpled look about her that I had learned to recognize in those media types. I walked up to her as she stood staring out of that window. I said, "Hi, my name is Ken."

Before I could finish, she turned to look at me and in an emotional whisper said, "Oh, Bom-bee." Now that "memory" is truly the answer to a prayer.

Today Cissy lives in the Portland, Oregon, area. We are again good buddies and she still calls me Bom-bee. She once told me of looking for my name in every telephone book she could find while she was growing up. Once she even told her teacher when asked who she most wanted to meet—what rock star or movie star. Cissy said she wanted to meet her dad more than anyone else in the world.

Ken "Duke" Monse'Broten

THE IN SIDE

Reprinted by permission of Matt Matteo.

Choices, Decisions, Consequences

Inside each of us lies dark and light. It is our choices that determine our fate.

David Smith

An examination of my psychological profile reveals that I have the same background as many pathological sex offenders, violent gang members and even murderers. If I had followed my anger and bitterness, I would now be spending the rest of my life in prison as an inmate. Instead I direct a nonprofit ministry that teaches inmates and their families how to attain true freedom.

I grew up in a small town nestled between the mountains of Virginia, with a mother who believed in extremely rigid discipline. My dad was a good man—a workaholic whose income only allowed us to live on what some considered the "wrong side of the tracks." Physically, I was always on the large side and somewhat clumsy. I soon became labeled as the "class punching bag"—a name that was used as an excuse for a fellow student to sexually assault me during an eighth-grade gym class. As a result, I spent the next two years bouncing in and out of doctors' offices and hospital rooms.

One evening I "died" in the back of a 1953 Cadillac ambulance as it raced toward the emergency room. The last thing I remember seeing, as I entered the dark tunnel, were headlights fading in the distance as the driver shoved the ambulance into second gear. It accelerated as fast as its big engine allowed. Moments later I found myself completely engulfed by a brilliant white light. A voice said, "It's not your time yet." I awoke in a hospital bed surrounded by people working feverishly to save my life.

The injury left lasting scars, most of which are invisible to the naked eye. One of the doctors who treated me also abused me. Nobody suspected it at the time because I was alone with him during the numerous "treatments" he called a medical routine.

The high fever that caused my "death" left me sterile and unable to memorize. My grades suffered in school, and I was told that I wasn't smart enough to go to college. I clowned around in an effort to find someone who cared but spent most of my time alone. My high school senior class rewarded my efforts by voting me to be the one "most likely to fail." I felt satisfied at my twenty-fifth-year reunion when I showed them my fifth published book, *As Free as an Eagle: The Inmate's Family Survival Guide.*

Breaking the chains that bound me to my past bitterness was a long journey. I learned that true freedom is not freedom from temptation or freedom from prison. True freedom is having the power to stop doing things that get us into trouble. One of the primary differences between adults and children is the ability to act on reason instead of emotional feelings. For me, attaining the freedom to become "somebody" meant I had to make a choice not to follow my own anger and bitterness. I had to ignore my inner voice saying, *You're worthless,* and replace it with an empowering voice saying, *You're worthwhile.*

I didn't do it alone. My journey toward freedom started

with my decision to select appropriate friends. Instead of associating with the "tough guys" who encouraged me to teach others to "respect" me by force, I chose to accept the help of people who taught me positive ways to handle anger. Two eighth-grade teachers and one assistant principal helped me negate and survive the hurtful words of classmates and teachers.

During my navy days, I chose going to church instead of "running" with the sailors who frequented the bar scene. "Mom and Pop" Marshall, a pastor and his wife, had a positive influence and "adopted" me into their family. I listened to those few educators who encouraged me to apply to college, instead of believing the results of the psychological tests predicting my failure. With the encouragement of a handful of supporting people and sheer determination, I learned to compensate for my inability to memorize. I earned two graduate degrees and became an ordained Baptist minister, a Licensed Professional Counselor and a Certified Family Life Educator.

We empower ourselves when we follow the road to freedom instead of getting caught in the revolving door of our past. Listening to people who believe in our abilities helps us find the power within ourselves to do better. Modeling positive people helps us create good choices and decisions, and changes negative consequences into positive outcomes.

Daniel Bayse

When we find ourselves facing a difficult decision, more often than not, life dictates that the choice we find least attractive is the correct one.
George Roth

It's What's Inside That Matters!

If you judge people you have no time to love them.

Mother Teresa

At the beginning of my speaking career, I was desperate for speaking engagements. I joked that when I opened the refrigerator door and the light came on, I'd begin a fifteen-minute presentation.

A good friend of mine was working in the prison system in Pennsylvania as an advocate for about four years. She often invited community professionals into her classes for inmates. Needless to say, it was a struggle to get people to make the commitment. First of all was the speaker's fee. There was none. Second was the fear. "What? Me go into a prison?" Yet she did it every day. One day, she asked me if I would go with her and speak in the prison.

It puzzled me why they would want a motivational speaker there. How motivated should they get? I agreed to do it anyway. It's what makes me who I am—a person on a mission wherever people are.

I'll never forget this presentation. First the metal detectors. Then every door we walked through slammed shut and locked behind us. The deeper inside we went, the more locked doors were left behind us. *I'll never get out in a hurry!* I thought. It reminds me of making a commitment in life. You take the first step to make the necessary changes. You close the door behind you and the further you go, the longer you remain committed, the more it becomes a part of who you are.

As I walked in the room, I saw men no different than me, except for the choices they had made in life. Suddenly, I knew why I committed myself to be there. I decided to speak to them no differently than I would to any other audience. I began by telling them that we had something in common.

"We are all prisoners," I proclaimed.

"You have walls you can see and measure. My prison is created in my mind and the limitations are set by me."

I continued by telling them I didn't care why they were there. That I was more concerned about who they were as human beings. One man in the back raised his hand and stood up and quoted Dr. Viktor Frankl—". . . everything can be taken from a man but one thing: the last of the human freedoms—to choose one's attitude in any given set of circumstances, to choose one's own way."

That began a discussion like no other I ever experienced. I closed my presentation the way I always do. "My name is Bob Perks and I believe in YOU!" I stepped into the crowd and repeated "I believe in you!" while shaking everyone's hand. My friend, amazed at the response, had this nervous giggle every once in a while. As we left the prison, nearly speechless, she stopped outside the main gate to say, "Thanks." I had asked her not to tell me anything about the crimes these men committed. But curiosity made me ask about the wonderfully intelligent gentleman who quoted Frankl. "Murder. Several people," she said. "But today he's one of the most incredible inmates. He's studying for a degree, serves the others in meeting their spiritual needs and works in the library. And he's here for life."

He has broken through the prison in his mind, but will never beat the walls that now hold him captive. But even sadder than this are the people who can go anywhere they want in this world but remain prisoners of their own minds.

Robert C. Perks

Wake Up to Life

Life isn't about finding yourself. Life is about creating yourself.

George Bernard Shaw

Has your very foundation ever been shaken by one of life's wake-up calls? Have you ever found yourself in the midst of a crisis that forced you to look at where your life was heading?

On April 19, 1991, I was arrested in my home in front of my two-year-old son. Tears were trickling down his cheeks as he watched his daddy being searched by masked, armed policemen and then handcuffed and taken away. That was my life's first wake-up call.

On January 3, 1992, I stood before a judge, facing a maximum, mandatory sentence of twenty-seven years. I trembled as I awaited sentencing. I looked around the courtroom, overcome with shock, shame, loneliness and fear. What had I done to myself? What had I done to my family, my three little boys, and my mother and dad? Why had I allowed my life to take this direction?

"Do you have anything to say, Mr. Rodriguez, before I

take your life into my hands?" the judge asked.

"Your honor, I . . . I . . . I'm. . . ."

"Guilty, guilty, guilty you are as you stand here. I command your physical body over to the Department of Correction for the next six years of your natural life. And I hope, sir, that you do a lot of thinking about where your life is headed. If I ever see you again in my courtroom, I'll make sure you stay an additional fifteen mandatory years in Delaware's best prison."

That was my life's second wake-up call.

He said to think, and think I did in those enclosed cement walls. You and I may be of different races, cultures, nationalities and economic status, but we have one thing in common. It doesn't matter whether you were born and raised in the largest slum in Puerto Rico, like my father; or whether you were born in Anchorage, Alaska, on an air force base, like me. It doesn't matter whether you wear prison coveralls, business suits or designer dresses; we all have one thing in common. We are all living, breathing, human beings. We all have the precious gift of life.

Where we lose our commonality is the manner in which we use this gift. Each of us was conceived by destiny, produced by purpose and packaged with potential to live a meaningful and fulfilling life. Deep within each of us lies a seed of greatness waiting to be germinated. Deep within us lies endless potential. Deep within us lie natural talents and gifts to manifest this potential.

What is it then that prevents us from becoming the person that our Creator intended us to be? Lack of self-confidence is a malaise that prevents many incredibly talented people from becoming all they can be. They don't believe that they have it in themselves to be what they want to be, and so they try to make themselves content with something less than they're capable of.

It took two drastic wake-up calls for me to realize that

there's only one quality that has had more of an effect on my life, and that's not believing in myself. Two drastic wake-up calls forced me to realize that I was teetering on the brink of disaster. It took those two alarms to go off before I became fully conscious of where my life was headed.

Now I still ask myself these questions: *Have I assessed my life lately? Have I looked at where I've been? Have I looked at where I am now? Have I looked at where I'm going? Have I asked myself where I want to go?*

It's never too late to take charge of my life. Grandma Moses discovered her talent for painting while in her eighties. What do I need to become all that I can be? What do I need to cultivate that seed of greatness? I need dreams, goals, commitment and ambition. It's deadly to become complacent.

Abraham Lincoln had incredible ambition. I need a curious mind, an insatiable desire to learn. Lincoln would walk miles just to borrow a book.

I need a positive outlook on life and faith in myself. Norman Vincent Peale accomplished many things in life, but not until he overcame his lack of faith in himself.

I need faith in a higher power. Moses led his people out of slavery, knowing that God would be with him to help carry out this mandate.

I need love and concern for my fellow humans. No one is an island. I need to see opportunities and have the courage to pursue them. I can't be afraid to take risks. I need to assess my life now and then to be sure I'm on the right track.

My wake-up calls were dreadful ones. Your wake-up call doesn't have to be as drastic as mine. Your wake-up call could be right here and right now.

In 1992, I stood before a judge, and I realized then what I had done with my life, and how carelessly I had used my precious gift. Hopefully, the next time I stand before a judge, it will be before my creator. He will ask about the gift of life that he gave me and say, "What did you do with it?"

When I tell him, may he be able to say to me, "Well done, thou good and faithful servant. Enter the kingdom of Heaven."

Kevin Scott Rodriguez

Empty pockets never held a man back. Only empty heads and empty hearts can do that.

Norman Vincent Peale

Teachers of Peace

*If there is to be any peace it will come through
being, not having.*

Henry Miller

On graduation night, each inmate received a certificate
identifying her as a "Teacher of Peace."

During our ceremony, we asked a few students to give
a testimony on their experience in class. One inmate
shared her feelings. "Teacher of Peace is the only label
I've ever had that is positive. I've been labeled prisoner,
criminal, low life, drug addict, unfit mother, thief, and
prostitute . . . all of which were true. This class has taught
me that, although there was some truth to those negative
identities, they weren't the whole truth. I'm more than
that now."

Each class of the seven-week Visions of Prisons program has a theme: Awareness, Acceptance, Meditation,
Mind Tools, Loss & Grief, Attitudinal Healing and Self-
Love. These steps are designed to replace a prisoner's
negative labels with a new, positive identity. The stigma
of negative labels diminishes our ability to rise above our

situation. We need to empower ourselves by replacing every former label with a positive one. Teacher of Peace is a label that works in prisons, at work, with our children or anywhere.

One student told us, "I had an argument last week where the other girl tried to get me into a fight. Believe me, before this class, she would have been sorry. Of course, I would have ended up in 'the hole' for thirty to sixty days, if I fought her, so I would have been sorry, too. I kept saying to myself, 'What she says isn't worth a hoot. I won't react to her.' She kept getting madder and madder, while I became calmer and calmer. I stood there receiving her negative energy, converting it and sending her back positive, loving energy. My friends, watching this in the dorm, said they could feel my peace. After a few minutes, the girl stopped attacking me and walked away.

"Later that night she came to my dorm and apologized. I was sitting meditating and thinking about her. I felt good about the way I handled the situation. When I opened my eyes, there she was in front of me again. Only this time, she had her hand extended saying, 'I'm sorry.'"

Dan Millstein

Focus Your Energy

Trials, temptations, disappointments—all these are helps instead of hindrances, if one uses them rightly. They not only test the fiber of character but strengthen it. . . . Every trial endured and weathered in the right spirit makes a soul nobler and stronger than it was before.

James Buckham

Dr. Viktor Frankl, author of *Man's Search for Meaning,* was one of the few survivors of Auschwitz. He was a German Jewish psychiatrist who somehow managed to live where tens of thousands of others died. With little food or clothing and no medical attention, he was forced to stand by while his fellow prisoners were cremated.

Upon being released at war's end, he was asked how he had managed to survive. What powers did he have that others lacked? How had he managed to stay alive?

He is said to have replied, "I always knew that my attitude was my own choice. I could choose to despair or to be hopeful. But to be hopeful I needed to focus on something I wanted.

"I focused on my wife's hands. I wanted to hold them one more time. I wanted to look into her eyes one more time. I wanted to think that we could embrace again and be heart to heart one more time. That kept me alive second by second by second."

Dr. Frankl did not have more energy available to him than the others at Auschwitz. He said that frequently his entire food ration was one pea in a bowl of soup. But rather than uselessly expend that energy in despairing at what was happening to him and those around him, he focused it on a single goal. He gave himself a reason to survive, and by concentrating on that reason, he was indeed able to survive.

Jack Canfield and Mark Victor Hansen

The List

God supplies us with all the talent, skill and ability necessary for achievement and success.

Curt Boudreaux
The ABC's of Self-Esteem

As a child, my parents used to tell me I could do anything. Then they'd say, "You're better than everyone else." That's a great responsibility. I did fine, until high school. Smart kids were labeled uncool. Struggling to fit in, I found an activity where I could shine—I could do drugs better than everyone else. In fact, I did drugs so well that when I graduated, I earned an all-expense paid, six-month vacation in the county jail.

I limped into my cell, a terrified nineteen-year-old heroin addict. After my body weaned itself off the drugs, my loneliness took over. I wanted the women there to like me so I told jokes, made fun of the guards and acted silly. I spoke my mind and earned myself a hero's reputation. I wrote poetry for the women to send to their lovers and children.

And so I gained the respect and friendship of my cellmate, Vicki, the leader of the biggest, meanest gang.

One hot Sunday, I was visiting another cell. They were giving each other tattoos. I didn't want to look wimpy, so I agreed to having my friend, Patty, give me a small one on the back of my shoulder.

When I returned to my cell, Vicki asked, "Where've you been?"

I started to climb up to my bunk, "Next door. Why?"

She demanded, "Don't you know by now I know everything that goes on in here? Let me see it."

"See what?"

"Show me, or else."

I swallowed hard. With my free arm, I slipped my shirt off my shoulder.

Vicki shouted, "You're so smart. Why do you do such stupid stuff?" She pushed her finger hard against my tattoo. "Don't you know this is poison? It can get in your blood. Then you die. If you don't care, why should I?" She pushed me off the bed onto the floor.

I rolled over and sobbed, "You're right. I'm so stupid. I can't do anything . . . my whole life is one big stupid failure."

As I raised my head, Vicki's palm pressed into my chest. "Stop it," she said.

I gasped, my voice splintering under the force of her palm.

She leaned her face into mine. "You may do stupid things," she said. "But *you* are not stupid. You're smart. You're strong." She released the pressure, but left her palm pressing against my skin. "And for some reason only known by God, you care about people."

Vicki sat back on her bunk. I blinked, not knowing what to say. She pointed at me and said, "That's what you've got to learn, that you aren't what you've done. When you get that in here," she pointed at her heart, then pointed out the door, "you'll get out of here."

There was nothing for me to say. All I could do was place her words in my brain to remember.

I listed Vicki's words on a piece of paper so I could keep them in my pocket as well as in my heart. I was released two months later. Vicki's words continued to echo in my ears. When I faced doing drugs again, I remembered her words, "You're smart. You're strong. God knows you care."

Instead of doing drugs, I returned to school. Three years later I graduated summa cum laude before returning home to earn a position as a corporate trainer. Whenever I felt fear, Vicki's words echoed again to remind me of my strengths. I kept a list of what made me special, and continued adding to it year after successful year.

Today, armed with two master's degrees and almost two decades of corporate work, I run a successful business providing seminars and personal coaching to help people be their best. No matter who comes to me for help, I have each person make a list of their personal list of powers to carry with them through difficult times. This process is a gift I love to share—a gift I learned from an angel named Vicki.

Marcia Reynolds

The Feeling of Success

*Somewhere between SUPPOSED TO and WANT
TO exists the still, small voice of reason that some
call conscience, but which I call God. It is when
we heed that voice that life becomes less complicated and our purpose becomes clearer.*

George Roth

While I was the warden of both the Huron Valley
Women's and Men's Prisons, I had the opportunity to
watch prisoners better their lives by becoming involved
in as many programs and activities as possible. Their talents brought enjoyment to employees and other prisoners as well. The woman who was the activities therapist
for the mentally ill inmates at the men's prison was able
to get a local director to help produce *The Caine Mutiny.*

Of all the prison productions, the most memorable was
the court scene acted by the mentally ill male prisoners
from maximum security. All employees, myself included,
were amazed that prisoners who could not get through a
day without their medications performed as well as any
professional—especially Tucker.

The first time I met Tucker, he was in his cell in a protective environment unit, which was the last one of several mental health units, each decreasing in intensity, before a prisoner was returned to general population. Tucker stood next to the cell door, facing the window on the opposite side of the room, throwing his filled laundry bag at the window. Once it landed, Tucker walked across the cell, picked up the laundry bag, returned to his position by the cell door and threw it at the window again. He repeated this over and over for several minutes until I asked him what he was doing.

"I can't sit still. I work in the kitchen on second shift. 'Til it's time for me to go, I gotta keep movin'."

All the time he talked to me, he paced back and forth in front of the cell door. Later, I discussed his case with the psychologist who explained, "Even on medication, Tucker is so hyper that he can hardly sleep, let alone sit still."

The psychologist couldn't convince Tucker that he could not be in the play because he was unable to stay still. Tucker begged and pleaded until she and the director gave in and let him play the part of one of a panel of judges.

I remember her instructions to him on opening night. "Don't forget, Tucker, if you cannot sit still and must move around, just get up and walk off the stage as if it is part of the play. No one will know the difference."

"I won't hafta do that. I know I can do this. I know I can."

Do it he did. He sat through the entire play, except for making periodic notes as a judge would. I can still recall the thrill I felt that night, as if I was watching my own child.

To this day, I think that somehow corrections and other agencies have missed the boat. We have not been able to capture whatever inner desire it was that made Tucker calm that night. He wanted to be in that play so much, he did whatever it took to be successful. As I watched him perform, I wondered why he and others like him couldn't succeed in real life. At least for the nights he performed in that play, Tucker was a success and escaped the internal horror that held him. Like me, many people in corrections continue to look for ways to replicate Tucker's encounter so that every incarcerated soul can experience the same exhilarating feeling of success.

Tekla Dennison Miller

*P*rison need not be the end of the road, but the beginning of an interesting and productive life.

Dr. Karl Menninger

8

ON WISDOM

Wisdom comes more from living than from studying.

Anonymous

THE IN SIDE

Reprinted by permission of Matt Matteo and Jerry Gillies.

The Unmaking of a Man

When I was a kid growing up in the mean streets of Harlem, I witnessed many fights. This helped develop my love for the sport of boxing. Sometimes when I'm sitting ringside watching a fight, it takes me back to when I was caught deep within one—in the confusing maze of streets.

Oftentimes I was heading for trouble and rarely in the direction of success. This lack of direction led many of the guys to prison instead of high school. Many of them were caught up in a cycle that still continues.

I remember the bravado of some guys that made it back to the outside. They talked about how they "handled" themselves in the joint. How they learned to fight good with their hands. No one ever came back and admitted that they were just plain scared. Instead, they hid behind huge muscles, thinking this proved they were real men. They were brutally baptized with deep scars to prove it.

I've always been fascinated by the whole concept of "proving oneself." Most of the time this is done ultimately in some type of battle. On the streets, it's manifested in fights, gang violence and murder. I had a lot of friends that went on this field trip and most stories were of glory, but some were of shameful defeat.

I started a correspondence with a prisoner doing forty-five years. He paints a picture of the joint as an environment that necessitates a tremendous psychological preparedness—a place where your life is always at stake. Michael Santos entered prison when he was about twenty-three. He's been behind bars for over twelve years now. In that time, he has worked toward rehabilitating himself, earning his bachelor's and master's degrees, and working on a Ph.D. He's quite respected for his academic accomplishments, both inside and outside prison, and has written extensively about the prison environment.

I'll share what he wrote to me about the everyday nuances of prison life, specifically that of predator and prey. But first, you better put your mouthpiece in good and lace your gloves real tight. Then make sure you've got your back against a wall as you're about to enter another kind of ring where the fights are oftentimes deadly—a place where there is very little chance of ever being a champion. This is real, and there is no bell to stop the action, and the last thing you want to be is knocked out.

A key to violence in prison is the length of time that prisoners are serving. In medium- and high-security prisons, individuals are serving well over ten years, with many who have no release dates at all. Low-security prisons hold primarily prisoners that have fewer than three years to serve. So there is still a connection with society. Their sentencing has a foreseeable end and is really regarded as punishment, an interruption in their lives. Long-term prisoners (ten years and up) come in with different attitudes. The environment supports a feeling of permanence. The prisoner can't make plans for the future because he sees no future. He eventually looks to receive "jailhouse respect," if he can operate inside the system and get things done. This can be by way of a gambling ring, drug distribution, food supply, smuggling, etc. And because many longtimers know that they will never be able to earn respect from society or from prison administrators, they choose to enhance their own status with other long-term offenders.

Prison is a society unto itself. It has its own heroes and leaders. But many long-term prisoners have rejected society, as society has rejected them. They must deal with the situation at hand, and it is a violent one. It's easy to earn a reputation as a dangerous prisoner. All one has to do is show that he is ready and willing to use violence to the extreme when anyone crosses him. For instance, a man was stabbed through the heart with a wooden stake (a shank) made from a broken mop handle because he said that he wouldn't pay a gambling debt of two dollars. Despite the violence of all of this, the murder was not about the two dollars; it was about perceived respect. Perception is of paramount importance in prison. The long-term prisoner has nothing else. He does not have a career, a house, a car, fancy clothes or anything else to distinguish himself. We have been raised from childhood, observing the importance of material possessions. It remains a warped basis for this new way of life.

This adverse environment is one where the more powerful a person is, the more respect he receives, from both staff and inmates. The staff will placate him by giving him a single cell to keep him calm, while assisting them in the keeping of order. Those who can't achieve status in any other way frequently become predators, aspiring to become known as a dangerous convict. It is a label many try to earn during the beginning years of their terms. If successful, he will be left alone, protected by a *reputation to murder. Cons will seek his favor or try to emulate him by exploiting others. The "others" are called "targets" or prey. Once marked as such, a convict's life is nearly worthless, as his possessions will be stolen, and he will be disrespected at every opportunity with relentless violence.*

With no one to turn to for "real" assistance, his weakness overwhelms him and he eventually submits to the lowest realms of man's inhumanity to himself. Once problems of this magnitude arise, there is very little chance of escaping without further complications to one's life. It's worse than your scariest nightmare, where sleep is something you take a chance on doing, at the risk of never waking up. A vicious circle that could go on for years or forever. For survival, you're caught up in a game that on either side will cost you some large part of whatever is left of your human decency.

Michael has used his time wisely in the joint, mostly by staying alert and being lucky. He has educated himself and found in that a new and productive beginning. Few prisoners reach such an analytical level, about themselves and their environment. It brings to the forefront the whole issue of rehabilitation. Is it really possible, and is it recognized by society? Does society understand what they create in the men they wear down by time? The whole concept of punishment seems to teach offenders how to effectively *not* be a part of society—the "unmaking" of a man.

Marion Boykin
Submitted by Laura Lagana

Punishment

To live continually in thoughts of ill will, cynical in suspicion of everyone, is to be confined in a self-made prison hole.

James Allen
As a Man Thinketh

It's impossible to escape the ever-present feeling of punishment during the initial months of imprisonment. I remember the sleepless nights, the contemplation of suicide, the humiliation I felt at being considered less than a person. The punishment was like a loud and continuous scream—one from which I couldn't escape. It was so loud that it shook me. But, as the days turned into weeks, then months and years, I began to get used to confinement. It was as if the scream of punishment had weakened to a faint whisper, one that takes some effort to hear. And so, time as punishment had lost its meaning, at least for me.

Prison, unfortunately, has become the only world I know. Although I maintain close ties with many people outside, relationships seem so distant, as if there's something fundamentally different between other people and me. My reality doesn't include the same activities or events as theirs. I know nothing about careers, significant others, children, voting, intimacy, travel or most other parts of life that people take for granted. Likewise, they understand little about the ways that I cope with confinement.

Time is all I have. After more than ten years of exile, it's become easy for me to accept that nothing will change except the seasons, and even they follow a cycle. One day just blends in with the next. There are no surprises. Nothing is new. I know that five years from today I'll be doing the same thing that I was doing five years ago, which is the same thing I'm doing today. I won't recognize or feel the punishment, but I'll be doing time.

It's odd to me that so many people think that time is an effective punishment. Perhaps I've become delusional. Maybe I am being punished after all. Can a man be punished if he doesn't know it? I can't tell anymore, because I don't know any other life besides the life that I'm living.

I remember the punishment phase, but for me, that phase ended long ago. In my case, that phase began immediately after my conviction. For most inmates, I think punishment begins immediately after the arrest. Things were different for me because I was naive. I listened to lawyers who promised me that, with the right amount of money, everything would be all right. My conviction was like a sudden and violent assault. When the jury returned to the courtroom and announced that I was convicted on every count, I was stunned and mortified. I felt thousands of daggers of guilt continuously being thrust into me. That guilt was punishment.

Punishment was the short ride from the courthouse to the jail, which seemed like eternity. It was realizing that chains and walls could hold me for so many years. Punishment was knowing that for decades I'd be living among society's outcasts, and then realizing that I was no different than them. I was an outcast, a convicted felon to be locked away with the other dregs of society.

Punishment was having to admit to my family that I was not only a convict, but a liar too. It was knowing that I disappointed my community and I humiliated everyone who believed in me. Punishment was realizing that I was a failure and that, as a convicted felon, I'd be branded the rest of my days. Punishment was being judged and controlled by people who thought they were better than me. Worse yet it was knowing that they were right.

Michael G. Santos

Often those who win at the justice game, lose at life. They "get off" and therefore never confront the real problems of their lives. In fact "winning" in court can harden people even more. They are never forced to stop and truly evaluate their lives. By winning, they lose.

Brian Brookheart
A Prisoner: Released

The Power of One

I am only one man but . . .

There was a man who spent his life in poverty. He was born to humble parents and never traveled further than two hundred miles from his home, yet he had an impact upon mankind that has never been equaled. His name was Jesus.

I am only one man but . . .

There was a man who believed that people should be free. He denied himself the many luxuries of life, even though he possessed a college degree that allowed him to practice law. Because of him, millions of his fellow countrymen were able to rid themselves of foreign colonial oppression. His name was Gandhi.

I am only one man but . . .

There was a man who took to heart the words of Abraham Lincoln that "All men are created equal." His belief in civil disobedience and nonviolent social change led an entire nation to a rebirth. His name was Martin Luther King Jr.

I am only one man but . . .

There was a man who spent nineteen years in prison doing hard labor because he believed his fellow countrymen deserved equal rights. His beliefs had him branded a "traitor" and yet, despite torture and deprivation, his faith was so strong that after nineteen years of inhumane treatment, he became the president of a new, free republic. His name is Mandela.

It is true that I am only one man, but . . .

I CAN MAKE A DIFFERENCE!!!

Gary K. Farlow

While You Were Out

"While you were out," read the memo my wife sent. It's the kind of message one might receive in an office. It was addressed to me, and the message was from the free world. I read on and pieced it together from the assortment of checked boxes.

While you were out, Mr. Cyan-Brock, the free world called and wishes you to return its call. The box labeled "Message" was also checked, and it read, "While you were out, some people lived their entire short lives. While you were out, more people were born than died. While you were out, wars were fought, won and lost, governments were overthrown, powers rose and fell, land masses shifted, and volcanoes erupted.

While you were out, whole nations of people starved to death while others destroyed their excess crops. While you were out, gold medals were won, medicines were discovered and people died because they didn't have insurance or money. While you were out, some animals became extinct; others were saved. While you were out, justice was served as often as it wasn't.

While you were out, your child grew into manhood without hearing your voice and your daughters rallied. While you were out, music changed forms and nearly four hundred songs hit the Billboard *number-one spot. While you were out, stories were written and told, and filmed and viewed by millions worldwide. While you were out, organ harvesting became common. While you were out, technology advanced, and video cameras and cash machines sprang up everywhere, while the number of working poor grew.*

While you were out, heroes were forged, victims abused and martyrs destroyed. While you were out, your family missed you. While you were out, people followed madmen to their doom and scoffed at the wise. While you were out, your wife changed from a young woman to a matron without you by her side. While you were out, so much happened that needed your attention. Please call back soon. The free world needs you.

Toni K. Cyan-Brock

Happy Holidays

People are as happy as they make their minds up to be.

Abraham Lincoln

In prison, holidays are the worst. Birthdays, anniversaries, Thanksgiving, Christmas, even Valentine's Day can be a "bummer." It's difficult and painful to be away from those we love—to be left out of the celebrations and the memory making. Many times, we feel a little forgotten or overlooked.

Birthdays in prison come and go without the comfort of cake with candles and the magic of blowing them out. Christmas mornings are without a fancy tree or presents. Thanksgivings are hard to feel thankful for, with dinner served on a cold, metal cafeteria tray.

My first Thanksgiving in prison, I refused to eat. My first birthday I spent alternating between rage and feeling more sorry for myself than ever before. On Christmas, I wouldn't even get out of bed. I stayed under the covers to hide the tears I cried all day.

So holidays in here are the worst—at least I thought

they were until I realized a few things. Once I stripped away all the commercialism and hype, I saw what holidays were all about. They're elaborate excuses we use to take a look at our lives, our successes and failures, and to spend quality time with our loved ones.

In here or out there, we can still take stock of ourselves and make plans, dream dreams, examine our behavior to see what we like and don't like. Even in here, we have the power to change what falls short of our ideal self-image.

Not being able to spend quality time with those we love is a little tougher—until we realize that the people we care for are always with us—in our hearts and minds. And just as they're with us, we are with them in spirit.

The days we can't spend together physically, we can still take time to remember them fondly . . . making phone calls, sending cards or letters helps both us and our loved ones.

Other people don't make us happy. Special places and people might help the mood, but the celebration and love comes from within. The challenge is to find it there—a state of mind, a positive attitude. It's easy to use a holiday as an excuse to be sad or edgy. I've been there. Our challenge is to celebrate every day as special. Life is a precious gift, whether we're in jail or not.

I'm planning a celebration every day this year—a celebration of life. You're invited. Happy Holidays! RSVP.

Daryl D. Foley

THE IN SIDE

Reprinted by permission of Matt Matteo.

The Wisdom of Jesse

Preconceived notions are the locks on the door to wisdom.

Merry Brown

My family drove ten hours, all the way from San Benito, Texas, to Oakdale, Louisiana. They were my first visitors while I was in the federal prison.

I knew this wouldn't be an easy visit because I had been in prison before, and had promised never to come again. I wanted to be at my best, so I got a fresh haircut and a clean shave. I even stayed up late the night before to starch and iron my prison khakis.

When I entered the visiting room that morning, my heart was pounding. My seven-year-old grandson, Jesse, burst from the crowd and hugged me like a young bear cub. My wife, Olga, and daughter, Joanne, followed, and lavished more hugs and kisses on me than I can ever recall receiving at one time.

My thoughts raced back to the day of my arrest. My family was angry then, but today I would make it better with my convict philosophy that says, "Crime is okay if you don't hurt anyone." I hadn't robbed, raped, or killed one living soul. I simply assisted in the transportation of drugs. My part in the offense was minor. Even the judge said so.

After I had my family gathered around me at one of the tables in the visiting area, I started defending my philosophy—a habit I learned in prison. "I'm a disabled American veteran," I said, even if I didn't really understand how that gave me license to violate the law. "I have the Purple Heart and enough other combat ribbons to cover half my chest. I killed people for this country and almost died in the process. Now what thanks do I get but another sentence?"

As I raged on and on, I noticed Olga and Joanne exchanging glances. I was angry and hurt. I knew that in just a little while my family would be going home and I would be staying. I wanted to cry. "I haven't hurt anyone!" I said it again, so loudly that those around us turned to stare.

I could see Olga's eyes fill with tears as Joanne looked away. Then, with tears streaming down his little cheeks, Jesse looked at me.

"What about me, Grandpa?"

As I looked down upon that little boy's face, it hit me. I have hurt someone. In fact, I have hurt the people who care about me the most. As visiting hour ended, I hugged my family one more time and they went home—without me.

Jesse Garcia

*P*retty much all the honest truth-telling there is in the world is done by children.

Oliver Wendell Holmes

Looking for Good

On the back of an envelope found among his effects after his death in a plane crash, former Atomic Energy Commission chairman Gordon Dean had scribbled: "Never judge people, don't type them too quickly; but in a pinch never first assume that a man is bad; first assume that he is good and that at worst he is in the gray area between bad and good."

Bob Considine

All convicts are evil low-lifes who deserve what they get. That's what I thought before I was sentenced to prison. I believed in tough treatment—feed them only bread and water. Forget about educational opportunities, heat, medical care, and certainly no TV or air conditioning— but what a difference time makes!

Now that I'm one of "them," I have a different view. I've met some genuinely nice, decent and responsible people who are "serving time."

The traditional view of inmates is that they're all career criminals who "feed on the public." They're heartless, irresponsible, uncaring, lower-income people from broken homes whose family and friends also have criminal records.

Admittedly, I carried my preconceived notions to prison. My first impressions confirmed all my fears. I was terrified by the experience and easily intimidated by practically everyone—inmates and staff alike.

Then an inmate, much older than I, pulled me aside and set me straight. I was obviously a first-timer and his advice helped me to survive. He introduced me to other inmates my own age. Thanks to their advice and guidance, I learned how to cope.

Many inmates are well educated, and most that aren't know its importance and are working on a GED or high school diploma to better themselves. Many fellow inmates have jobs in the prison. They work in the library, laundry, cafeteria, garden, canteen and educational building, and perform maintenance tasks for little or no pay. Most inmates are grateful to have jobs and take pride in their work. It helps build self-worth in a place where it's easy to feel worthless.

Like me, many of us have never been to prison before and never want to return. Many come from single-parent, middle-class families and are the first family member to serve a term. Most of their friends are law-abiding citizens.

Prison is a cold, cruel place, yet the inmates who helped me did so with nothing expected in return. Their advice saved my life and helped make the experience bearable.

It's true, people don't go to prison for being good. Most of us did something to deserve our time, but it doesn't mean that we're all bad. Looking for the good in everyone helps set us all free.

Clifford G. Angeroth

The Law of Compensation

If you commit a crime and are tried in court
And acquitted by a twist of a tort.
Are you really innocent of what you've done?
Even if the courts say you have won.
But that's not true, there's a universal law.
It works all the time without a flaw.
It's The Law of Compensation, there's a price to pay
Even if things seem to go your way.
There's a price internal for everything you do.
It must be paid no matter how you argue.
Harm someone, you'll know it within
Even if the courts say you shall win
You'll know in your heart, you're guiltier than sin.
So before you do anything, these questions ask
Even if it's a simple task.
Is this task wise? Will it hurt anyone?
Will everyone benefit when the task is done?
Will everyone say it's a Win/Win deal?
Will everyone be satisfied with how they feel?
Am I willing and able to pay the total price?
Will everyone be free of sacrifice?
If you can say YES to these questions,
You can be sure
Everyone will be winner,
Everyone will feel secure.

Sid Madwed

World Without Violence

If we are ever going to solve the problem of violence in our society, we're going to have to find ways that closed hearts can open and broken lives can mend.

Robin Casarjian
The Lionheart Foundation

The most important thing I learned from my grandfather was to recognize anger and deal with it positively. I was a very angry young man because of the racial beatings and humiliations I suffered in South Africa.

My grandfather taught me that "an eye for an eye" philosophy is not justice. That's revenge. Justice is when you're able to change people from their wrong ways through love and dialogue. He also taught me that anger is a good and powerful source of energy. Without some anger, we wouldn't be motivated to do anything.

Sometimes, though, we misuse that energy for negative purposes. To direct my anger positively, my grandfather taught me to write in an anger journal. This provided me a harmless way to express my anger, but more than this, it also challenged me to write a solution. This allowed me to use my anger without hurting anyone. It also gave me a written record of my emotions to analyze.

My grandfather's most important teaching is his philosophy of nonviolence. He explained it by challenging me to learn what "violence" truly is. He explained that unless we know what is wrong, it's difficult to recognize what is right. He told me to be aware of passive or nonphysical violence, such as hate, prejudice, oppression, intolerance and discrimination. In fact it's passive violence that fuels physical violence because it generates anger. Grandfather believed we can't create peace and harmony when we ignore passive violence.

Grandfather told me, "Our minds must be like a room with many open windows. Let the breezes blow in from all directions, but refuse to be blown away by any of them. Imagine a room that is airtight. There will soon be no oxygen and the room will be unlivable. This is what happens to a mind that is closed. When we open the windows of our room, we let in a lot of lifesaving oxygen and some impurities along with it. The good that the air does is so great that the bad is inconsequential."

He challenged me to set attainable goals and make continual progress to control my anger. We may not be able to eliminate all violence in the world, but we can reduce it significantly by respecting the diversity of each other. Imagine a world without violence.

Arun Gandhi

There are no problems in this world that we can't solve together.

Liz Sabo

Success—Who Can Judge?

While awaiting sentencing, I decided to give stand-up comedy a shot. The judge had suggested I get my act together, and I took him seriously.

Tim Allen

In September 1997, I coordinated a project to bring a group of motivational speakers into prison for Make-a-Difference Day. The warden had given me a list of specific criteria each speaker needed to meet in order to gain entrance to the prison for that program. The first item on that list was: "No criminal record."

I had volunteered in this prison for the past five years, and when I decided to coordinate this program, I had immediately thought of many potential speakers—including several former inmates. I had been especially excited about inviting one in particular to speak—Rick.

Rick had spent most of his adult life in prison. It appeared he was on the in-and-out plan. First he would be in, then he would be out—released just long enough to get himself sentenced to be in again. But two years earlier he had been released, and he had not returned. He finally found a way to become successful in society. I was proud of him. I believed his story could help make a difference to the current inmate population in a way no other motivational speakers could. After all, Rick had been there, and now he was a success—on the outside.

So I asked the warden to make an exception. "Obviously, he has found a way to live successfully and responsibly," I pleaded. "I'm sure his message could move these inmates like no one else's."

"Tell me the name again," the warden requested.

"Rick," I said, and I gave his full name.

"But Rick is in Booking right now—he was brought back in last night."

I felt my heart drop. I must have been wrong. Rick wasn't a success after all. He had been out of jail for two years—but now he was back. And probably for life. Hadn't the judge warned him at his last sentencing? If he was arrested and convicted again, he would be sentenced to a life term as a habitual criminal.

I was beyond disappointment. Part of me felt like chucking it all. *Make-a-Difference Day*, I thought. *Hummphh.* Apparently, nothing made a difference. But I kept working at the arrangements anyway—halfheartedly.

A week later, I ran into Rick at the weekly meeting I sponsor in the prison. I was both happy and sad to see him and greeted him with my standard big hug, and I told him how I felt.

"I was so sure you had made it! I was certain you were a success! What happened? I'm so disappointed."

Rick's answer surprised me: "But Tom, I *am* a success. In forty-four years, this is the longest time I have ever been out of jail. I was responsible! I paid my electric bills and phone bills—for two years! I have been clean, drug-free and sober for all this time. I did a stupid thing, yes. But that is nowhere near as stupid as the stuff I used to do. And I'm only sentenced to four months for a parole violation. Me? I can still walk with my head held high. I am a success."

I'm not ashamed to tell you that the next thing he said brought tears to my eyes. "Please don't be disappointed— so much of my success is because of you! The way you always showed up, week after week, and helped us put this program together. The way you always greeted me with a smile and genuine concern about how I was doing. The way you believed in me even when I couldn't believe in myself. Maybe those couple of hours every week weren't such a big deal to you, but to me, they were everything."

He was right. He was a success. He was a success because he saw himself as one. Rick had changed.

The funny thing was, now that Rick was back inside the walls, I didn't need any special permission to make him a speaker at the Make-a-Difference Day program. Maybe his parole violation actually served a greater purpose, after all. And as I listened to him, the truth dawned on me: Rick didn't need to wait the four months of his sentence to regain his freedom. His perception of himself had already set him free.

Tom Lagana

Not a Mistake

Life is a process of making mistakes, learning from them and making wise choices. No one is perfect, but we can become better with each new day when we are ready to learn.

Laura Lagana

In 1994 I did something that I'm ashamed of, and I served a three-year prison sentence. I realize there were a lot of people who hated me. I even hated myself for the mistake I made—for what I did, but not for who I am. Good people are sometimes capable of doing bad things and allow stupidity to overcome rational thought.

I blindly followed the wrong crowd. I'll live with that for the rest of my life, but I'm still a decent human being with ambitions, feelings and a vision for my future.

I share my story to help others live their lives in a more positive and meaningful way, instead of allowing poor judgment to destroy them. Even with endless talent and exceptional intellect, when we're unethical, we can lose everything we've worked hard to achieve.

I learned a lot from my prison experience. Without the

loving support of friends and family, life is meaningless. My prison sentence hurt my family and friends even more than it hurt me.

My three-year sentence was enough time to think about my mistake, but that's not enough punishment for me. I never want to serve another minute in prison, but I do want to spend my life serving my community.

It's not what we do occasionally that makes us who we are, it's what we do consistently. Good people sometimes do bad things. I'm no longer the same person I was in 1994. I made a mistake, but I'm not a mistake.

Juan Jose (Johnny) Galvan

The best way to see the good in others is to look for it in yourself.

Sandy Krauss
*Set Yourself Free: How to Unlock
the Greatness Within You!*

Wasted Time

The time that I've wasted is my biggest regret,
Spent in these places I will never forget.
Just sitting and thinking about the things that I've done,
The crying, the laughing, the hurt and the fun.

Now it's just me and my hard-driven guilt
Behind a wall of emptiness I allowed to be built.
I'm trapped in my body, just wanting to run
Back to my youth with its laughter and fun.

But the chase is over and there's no place to hide.
Everything is gone, including my pride.
With reality suddenly right in my face
I'm scared, alone and stuck in this place.

Now memories of the past flash through my head
And the pain is obvious by the tears that I shed.
I ask myself why and where I went wrong.
I guess I was weak when I should have been strong.

Living for the drugs and the wings I had grown,
My feelings were lost, afraid to be shown.
As I look at my past it's so easy to see
The fear that I had, afraid to be me.

I'd pretend to be rugged, so fast and so cool
When actually lost like a blinded old fool.
I'm getting too old for this tiresome game
Of acting real hard with no sense of shame.

It's time that I change and get on with my life,
Fulfilling my dreams for a family and wife.
What my future will hold I really don't know,
But the years that I've wasted are starting to show.

I just live for the day when I'll get a new start
And the dreams I still hold deep in my heart.
I hope I can make it, I at least have to try
Because I'm heading toward death, and I don't want to die.

Dave LeFave

Time-Out

Weekends, to many people, are an escape from a weekly prison of purposeless.

Denis Waitley
The New Dynamics of Goal Setting

"Where are you Grandma?" Asked Lori, one of my four-year-old twin granddaughters. "Grandma is on a giant time out," I told her gently. I couldn't think of any other way to explain where I was. I had just been sentenced to five years in prison and was calling home for the first time. It was difficult for my family, especially my grandchildren, to understand what had happened.

Time out is exactly what I have. A time to reflect on my life—where I had been, and where I want to go. When I was free, I wasn't sure who I was. My favorite question was, "What do I want to be when I grow up?" That sounds like a stupid question for a forty-four-year-old woman, but I didn't know what I wanted to do with my life.

Up to this point, I did what was expected of me. I was the superwoman—wife, mother, grandmother and professional career woman. Outwardly it appeared that I was succeeding. I was married for twenty years, had two grown daughters, four grandchildren, and a bookkeeping job for eight years. I had a home in the city and a log cabin in the north woods. I had everything. Why, then, did I feel like a failure and a fake?

This time-out has given me the opportunity to look at my life and examine my values and beliefs. Now I know what my priorities are. Family and friends are far more important than material things. I never thought that my life made a difference to anyone else. Like George in the movie, *It's a Wonderful Life*, I felt useless and alone. This time-out has shown me that I am special, and I do make a difference.

Instead of wandering aimlessly, not knowing what I want, I have set my life on course. Creating short- and long-term goals has given my life direction and purpose.

Even though I regret what I did to get this time-out, I am thankful for it. I now have the determination and self-esteem to accomplish my goals. I'm at peace with myself and can accept who I am, even though I may not succeed at every single thing. I know I'm not superwoman.

This experience has forced me to focus on healing myself spiritually and emotionally. I'll continue to take voluntary time-outs when I'm free, so I'll never have another mandatory time-out.

Sandra Keller

THE IN SIDE

When we have inner peace, we can be at peace with those around us. When our community is in a state of peace, it can share that peace with neighboring communities.

Dalai Lama

Who Is Jack Canfield?

Jack Canfield is one of America's leading experts in the development of human potential and personal effectiveness. He is both a dynamic, entertaining speaker and a highly sought-after trainer. Jack has a wonderful ability to inform and inspire audiences toward increased levels of self-esteem and peak performance.

He is the author and narrator of several best-selling audio and videocassette programs, including *Self-Esteem and Peak Performance, How to Build High Self-Esteem, Self-Esteem in the Classroom* and *Chicken Soup for the Soul—Live.* He is regularly seen on television shows such as *Good Morning America, 20/20* and *NBC Nightly News.* Jack has coauthored numerous books, including the *Chicken Soup for the Soul* series, *Dare to Win* and *The Aladdin Factor* (all with Mark Victor Hansen), *100 Ways to Build Self-Concept in the Classroom* (with Harold C. Wells) and *Heart at Work* (with Jacqueline Miller).

Jack is a regularly featured speaker for professional associations, school districts, government agencies, churches, hospitals, sales organizations and corporations. His clients have included the American Dental Association, the American Management Association, AT&T, Campbell Soup, Clairol, Domino's Pizza, GE, Hartford Insurance, ITT, Johnson & Johnson, the Million-Dollar Roundtable, NCR, New England Telephone, Re/Max, Scott Paper, TRW and Virgin Records. Jack is also on the faculty of Income Builders International, a school for entrepreneurs.

Jack conducts an annual eight-day Training of Trainers program in the areas of self-esteem and peak performance. It attracts educators, counselors, parenting trainers, corporate trainers, professional speakers, ministers and others interested in developing their speaking and seminar-leading skills.

For further information about Jack's books, tapes and training programs, or to schedule him for a presentation, please contact:

Self-Esteem Seminars
P.O. Box 30880
Santa Barbara, CA 93130
Phone: 805-563-2935
Fax: 805-563-2945
Web site: *http://www.chickensoup.com*

Who Is Mark Victor Hansen?

Mark Victor Hansen is a professional speaker who, in the last twenty years, has made over four thousand presentations to more than two million people in thirty-two countries. His presentations cover sales excellence and strategies; personal empowerment and development; and how to triple your income and double your time off.

Mark has spent a lifetime dedicated to his mission of making a profound and positive difference in people's lives. Throughout his career, he has inspired hundreds of thousands of people to create a more powerful and purposeful future for themselves, while stimulating the sale of billions of dollars worth of goods and services.

Mark is a prolific writer and has authored *Future Diary, How to Achieve Total Prosperity* and *The Miracle of Tithing*. He is coauthor of the *Chicken Soup for the Soul* series, *Dare to Win* and *The Aladdin Factor* (all with Jack Canfield) and *The Master Motivator* (with Joe Batten).

Mark has also produced a complete library of personal empowerment audio and videocassette programs that have enabled his listeners to recognize and use their innate abilities in their business and personal lives. His message has made him a popular television and radio personality, with appearances on ABC, NBC, CBS, HBO, PBS and CNN. He has also appeared on the cover of numerous magazines, including *Success, Entrepreneur* and *Changes*.

Mark is a big man with a heart and spirit to match—an inspiration to all who seek to better themselves.

Who Is Tom Lagana?

Tom Lagana is a professional speaker, author and engineer. He is a 1994 recipient of the Jefferson Award for Outstanding Public Service and a member of the International Federation of Speaking Professionals. With thirty-five years of experience in the corporate world, Tom works with successful teams throughout North America, Europe and the Far East.

As a professional engineer, Tom made periodic technical presentations. Recognizing the need to improve his public speaking skills, Tom turned to Toastmasters International. In 1992, two inmates inspired Tom to form a prison group, and seven years later the national award-winning Walking Tall Club continues to flourish.

While working on a special project for the warden in 1997, Tom visited a bookstore in search of motivational resources for the inmates to read. After seeing books similar to the *Chicken Soup for the Soul* series he began his own book of touching stories for inmates.

Months later, while attending Jack Canfield's Facilitation Skills Seminar in Santa Barbara, California, Tom mentioned his book to Jack Canfield. Jack replied that he and Mark Victor Hansen wanted a *Chicken Soup for the Prisoner's Soul* book but lacked someone to spearhead the project. Tom immediately volunteered.

For nearly three years, Tom collected and wrote prison-related stories. He continues to write to inmates and their loved ones, as well as prison staff, volunteers, and victims.

Tom presents Success Skills Seminars to inmates, prison staff and corporate clients. He has been happily married to Laura for more than thirty years. They have two grown sons and a grandchild.

For further information about Tom's training programs, or to schedule him for a presentation, please contact:

Success Solutions
P.O. Box 7816
Wilmington, Delaware 19803
E-mail: *TomLagana@yahoo.com*
Web site: *http://www.TomLagana.com*

Contributors

Candace F. Abbott is the founder of Delmarva Christian Writers' Fellowship. She is author of the book, *Fruit-Bearer.* Candy and her husband Drew are owners of Fruit-Bearer Publishing. She may be reached at P.O. Box 777, Georgetown, DE 19947; e-mail: *dabbott@dmv.com;* Web site: *http://www.angelfire. com/journal/fruitbearer.*

Ron Ambrosia is a born-again Christian, fifty-year-old native of Ohio. He has been incarcerated since 1988 and is serving a life sentence. He enjoys gardening, writing and participating in theatre by writing, acting, set construction and song. He is a graduate of Kairos, GOALS, and a member of Toastmasters. He may be reached at Marion Correctional Institution, #201252, P.O. Box 57, Marion, OH 43301-0057.

Clifford G. Angeroth is married, a career Bible student, and currently working on a collection of short stories. He may be reached at P.O. Box 733, Rock Hill, SC 29731-6733.

Perry Arledge is a speaker, humorist, dessert analyst and author of *People Are Just Desserts.* She is the owner of The Sweet Rewards Company, whose goal is to touch people with their own greatness. She can be reached at P.O. Box 152139, Austin, TX 78715, e-mail *srewards@aol.com;* Web site: *www.perrya.com.*

Cecilia Thomasson Baker is an administrative assistant for a large retail chain and an amateur writer. She may be reached at P.O. Box 391, Lubbock TX 79408-0391.

Neil Soriano Bagadiong is the assistant dean of student affairs at Ivy Tech State College-Anderson after six years in admissions at Ball State University in Muncie, Indiana. He received a bachelor's degree in communications and a master's degree in higher education administration, both from Purdue University. He is a national officer for Delta Sigma Phi Fraternity, coaches youth soccer and serves on the executive board for MDA of Central Indiana. He has collected three hundred pages of inspirational stories and believes in the enlightenment of the soul through education. He may be reached at e-mail: *nbagadio@ivy.tec.in.us*

Daniel J. Bayse, EdS, LPC, CFLE, SC, is the executive director of Prison Family Foundation Inc. This ministry provides counseling to inmates and their families locally, programs and training to prison systems worldwide. He may be reached at P.O. Box 12175, Huntsville, AL 35815; e-mail: *pffi@prodigy.net.*

Douglas Paul Blankenship is a builder-developer of luxury homes and commercial buildings. He is an international motivational speaker and author of *The Tour, Synchronized Conquest, Success Formulas, Love Is the Matter of the Heart* and numerous short stories and technical articles. He holds four degrees, including a Ph.D. He may be reached at 600 East Ocean Blvd., Suite 1003, Long Beach, CA 90802.

Kenneth L. Bonner is the founder and past president of Creative Attitudes Undertaking Self Education (CAUSE), a nonprofit self-help organization for prisoners who are committed to personal growth and positive change. His role models are Anthony Robbins, Les Brown and Stephen Covey. He may be reached at #104075, P.O. Box 5000 NECX, Mountain City, TN 37683-5000.

Kim Book is a prison volunteer in Delaware for Prison Fellowship Ministries, Pre-Release Program, Parenting Program, Personal Development Program and the Victim's Sensitivity Program. She is a trained mediator, mediating minor offenses for the district attorney's office. She is currently working on a program to do mediations between victims and offenders of violent crimes. She may be contacted at e-mail: *JOCKOKIM@aol.com*; Web site: *http://www. angelfire.com/de2/pf.*

Roy A. Borges is a prisoner in Florida writing for the Lord. He is a 1998 First-Place Amy Award Winner. He may be reached at #029381 WCI, 4455 Sam Mitchell Drive, Chipley, FL 32428.

Joan Borysenko, Ph.D., is a medical scientist, licensed psychologist and author of nine books on healing, spirituality, personal growth and women's issues. Her *New York Times* bestseller, *Minding the Body, Mending the Mind,* is a classic in the field of integrative medicine in which she is one of the pioneers. Please see her Web site: *http://www.JoanBorysenko.com.*

Curt Boudreaux is a professional speaker and author. He is a member of the National Speakers Association. He is the author of *The ABCs of Self-Esteem* and an audiotape entitled *The Keys To Unlocking Your Potential.* He is a twelve-year veteran of prison ministry work. Curt can be reached at P.O. Box 422, Golden Meadow, LA 70357, e-mail: *curtboudreaux@cajunnet.com*; Web site: *http://www. nolaspeaks.com/cb.*

Marion Boykin is a noted sports columnist/freelance writer in the New York City area. Currently, he is the sports editor for *The Black World Today* Web site *(www.tbwt.com),* and his commentary is regularly featured on the Internet there. He may be reached at e-mail: *Mb217@aol.com.*

R. Troy Bridges, one of the foremost meditation teachers in prison today, also leads Emotional Awareness groups, while serving a sentence of life without parole. His first book, *Spiral,* is due to be published soon. He may be contacted at 1949 Braddock Drive, Hoover, AL 35226.

Brian Brookheart is an envangelist, speaker, businessman and author. His book, *A Prisoner: Released,* has touched thousands of hearts for Christ. He is a featured platform speaker for Operation Starting Line, the largest prison outreach in America. He may be reached at Brian Brookheart Ministries, 44 Music Square East, PMB #509, Nashville, TN 37203; e-mail: *sbtower2@midwest.net*; Web site: *http://www.brookheart.com.*

Douglas Burgess is the editor of the prison newspaper, *The KCF Link,* at Kinross Correctional Facility. He is serving a life sentence for a crime he committed while on leave from the marine corps in 1984. He is a man committed to atoning for his past misdeeds through numerous programs benefiting homeless shelters, food banks and youthful offenders. He is currently earning a master's degree, learning another language and writing his second book. He may be contacted at #178559 Kinross Correctional Facility, 16770 S. Watertower Drive, Kincheloe, MI 49788.

Charles Carkhuff is an aspiring artist. He is an inmate at Snake River Correctional Institution. He writes poems and draws cartoons and greeting cards. He is interested in helping others reach their full potential and see their goodness. He may be contacted at #5916716, 777 Stanton Blvd., Ontario, OR 87914 or 304 Roosevelt #4, Klamath Falls, OR 97601.

Antoinette (Toni) Carter is a teacher in the Pre-Release Program at Folsom State Prison in Represa, CA. She has held various teaching positions in her ten years in the Education Department. In 1992, she received the Outstanding Academic Teacher of the Year Award. Toni is an active member of the Correctional Education Association and has served as chair of the Board of Trustees for her church for the past three years. Prior to coming to Folsom Prison, she taught for two years in the Detroit Public School System. She can be reached at P.O. Box 983, Roseville, CA 95678 or e-mail: *netnuts@quiknet.com.*

Rod Carter is the Ontario Regional Chaplain for the Correctional Service of Canada and an ex-offender. He received a criminal pardon in 1977. He is an adjunct faculty member at Queen's Theological College where he teaches in the area of Restorative Justice and Corrections; and Ministry in the Context of Violence. He may be reached at 710-140 Elliott Avenue, Kingston, Ontario K7K 6P1, Canada or e-mail: *Carterrs@csc-scc.gc.ca.*

George Castillo was a prison chaplain for more than twenty years. His book, *My Life Between the Cross and the Bars,* has inspirational stories of life-changing experiences which led him to advocate prison reform. He may be reached at G & M Publications, P.O. Box 657, Shalimar, FL 32579; e-mail: *g-mpub@gnt.net*; Web site: *http://www.angelcities.com/members/gmpub.*

Jay Cocuzzo may be contacted at #180963-D-1209-L, Okeechobee Correctional Institute, P.O. Box 1984, Okeechobee, FL 34973-1984.

Charles Colson was a well-known public figure, convicted and imprisoned for seven months due to his involvement in the Watergate scandal as Nixon's Special Counsel. A year after his release he started a prison ministry. In 1993, he was awarded the Templeton Prize for Progress in Religion. He is now a nationally recognized speaker and founder of Prison Fellowship.® Web site: *http://www.prisonfellowship.org/.*

Toni K. Cyan-Brock is the wife of an inmate. She is a mother and author of "Prisoners of Love: a guide for anyone wanting to maintain, strengthen and cultivate relationships with loved ones during times of incarceration," both a book and newsletter. She may be reached at P.O. Box 32531, Amarillo, TX 79120; e-mail: *Prisoners_of_love@yahoo.com*; Web site: *http://members.xoom.com/prisonoflove/.*

Jane Davis is a writer, international speaker and the founder of HOPE-HOWSE International, Inc., a nonprofit organization dedicated to creating peace through honesty, faith and action. Jane earned her AB in cultural anthropology and her master's degree in social work from Washington University in St. Louis. HOPE-HOWSE is an acronym for a philosophy: Help Other People Evolve through Honest Open Willing Self Evaluation. She may be contacted at HOPE-HOWSE; PMB 128; 4514 Chamblee-Dunwoody Rd.; Atlanta, GA 30338; Web site: *http://www.hope-howse.org/*; e-mail: *jane@hope-howse.org*.

Steven Dodrill is a photographer-turned-writer. He is interested in corresponding with anyone who appreciates the written word. He may be reached at e-mail: *harvey.gittler@oberlin.edu or* #187-143 (M-A), P.O. Box 740, London, OH 43140.

Judge Bob Downing has been a District Court judge since 1985. He is best known for his School or Jail program, which received national attention during the late 1980s (being covered by *People* and *Geraldo*). Seeing literacy and public speaking as important tools in inmate rehabilitation, Judge Downing started several Toastmasters Clubs behind bars. He may be reached at e-mail: *down@iamerica.net*.

Normandie Fallon, RN, is a registered nurse, working in hospitals for over thirty-three years. She and her husband, Tom, have volunteered through Prison Ministry at San Quentin for eight years, where they started an Overcomers group. It has been incredibly rewarding and a true blessing. She is currently working on more stories and a screenplay. She may be reached at P.O. Box 3574, Walnut Creek, CA 94598; e-mail: *normandief@hotmail.com*.

Colleen Fiant is the Business Administrator and a GOALS facilitator at Marion Correctional Institution in Marion, Ohio. She has completed two Associate degrees, a Bachelor's Degree, and is finishing her Masters in Business Administration. Her background is in Business Administration with a complimenting focus in human behavior. She may be reached at MCI, P.O. Box 57, Marion, OH 43302; e-mail: *blackgold@acc-net.com*.

Gary K. Farlow is a native tarheel with a juris doctorate from Heed University. He practiced law prior to entering prison in 1991. His works have appeared in two poetic anthologies, *Essence of a Dream* and *Best Poems of 1998*. His works, *Prisonese: A Dictionary of Prison Slang, Conferring with the Moon,* and *After Midnight: Two Volumes of Poetry,* may be ordered by writing Gary K. Farlow c/o Carolyn Jackson, 915 Benjamin Benson St., Greensboro, NC 27406.

Daryl D. Foley is a poet, musician and ex-con (among other things). He may be reached at *madpoetshelley@aol.com*.

Robert Fuentes is a thirty-nine-year-old Mexican, originally from Corona, CA. He is currently into his fifteenth year of a life sentence. His writings have appeared in several publications, including *Extracts from Pelican Bay* and

America's Best Poetry. He may be reached at C-88749, C-9-114, P.O. Box 7500, Pelican Bay State Prison, Crescent City, CA 95532.

Kathleen Gage is vice president of The Murdock Group and a member of the National Speakers Association. She is the author of the tape series *Living with Serenity* and *Confidence and Credibility Through High Self-Esteem*. She may be reached at e-mail: *kathleengage@themurdockgroup.com* Web site: *http://www. murdock.com.*

Juan Jose (Johnny) Galvan is currently on parole. He maintains a Web site for anyone interested in learning more about prison life. He is currently earning a management information systems (MIS) degree from the University of Texas at Austin. He may be reached through Web site: *http://firsttimefelon.com.*

Arun Gandhi is the president and cofounder of the M. K. Gandhi Institute for Nonviolence at Christian Brothers University, Memphis, Tennessee. He is the author of *World Without Violence*. He may be reached at 650 East Parkway South, Memphis, TN 38104; e-mail: *arungandhi@msn.com;* Web site: *http://www.cbu.edu/Gandhi.*

Jesse Garcia is a husband, father, grandfather, born-again Christian, served in Viet Nam, and is a disabled and decorated ex-Marine. He is now serving twenty years in prison. He may be reached at 925 Wentz St., San Benito, TX 78586.

Dale Gaudet is the coeditor of a Toastmasters newsletter that received the "Top Ten International Newsletter Award." He is an inspiring author, a twenty-one-year veteran in produce/floral marketing, and a single father of two teenage daughters. Dale is currently a Chaplain's clerk, achiever and avid speaker. He may be reached at 325242, Ash 2, Louisiana State Prison, Angola, LA 70712.

John W. Gillette Jr. is married for over twenty-three years and has five children. He is a graduate of Stanford University and is working on developing a Christian ministry devoted to teaching people about prayer anbd the deeper life in Christ. He is serving time in San Diego, California. He may be reached at #K83600, 1-2-10SU, 480 Alta Rd., San Diego, CA 92179.

Jerry Gillies is a former journalist (NBC-New York). He is the author of six books on personal development and relationships, including the bestselling *Moneylove* (Warner Books). For over twenty years, he conducted seminars and gave lectures across the U.S., Canada, England and South Africa. He is currently an inmate at a California state prison and may be reached at #K466460 FSP-B3/B1-11L, P.O. Box 715071, Represa, CA 95671-5071.

The **Billy Graham** Evangelistic Association would be glad to hear from you regarding your biblical questions, and also to assist you in accepting Christ as your Savior. You may reach them by calling the toll-free number 1-877-2graham, or by writing to Billy Graham, 1300 Harmon Place, Minneapolis MN 55403.

Gordon Graham is a powerful, electrifying speaker on change and its impact on people. He has been involved in staff and inmate training/education in correctional institutions across the U.S. and Canada for the past twenty-five years. His program, *A Framework for Breaking Barriers*, is one of the most effective cognitive change programs in the U.S. He may be reached at P.O. Box 3927, Bellevue, WA 98009; Web site: *http://www.ggco.com.*

Diane Harshman is a retired elementary school teacher. She has one son who is an elementary teacher in Orlando, FL. She maintains a close relationship with her friend and former student, the subject of her story. She may be reached at e-mail: *harshfl@hotmail.com.*

Efrain Frank Hernandez is a forty-four-year-old single father of two daughters and two grandsons. Frank is a director in the Gander Hill Prison's Pre-Release Program, where he encourages other inmates to make positive life-style changes. He may be reached at #158027 P.O. Box 9561, Wilmington, DE 19809.

Thomas Ann Hines is a Certified Criminal Justice Specialist. She raised her only child, Paul, as a single mother. Ms. Hines was a Certified Professional Electrologist, owning her own business for twenty-three years. Governor George Bush appointed her to the Private Sector Prison Industry Oversight Authority Board for a six-year term. She has received the highest volunteer award given by Governor Bush and awards from the Texas Department of Criminal Justice and the Texas Youth Commission. She has spoken in prisons and juvenile facilities since 1994. She has been a guest on the Oprah Winfrey show. She may be reached at P.O. Box 864499, Plano, TX 75086-4499, or e-mail: *TAHines@aol.com.*

Andre T. Jackson is an air force veteran of the Gulf War. He completed his first two novels, *Black Diamonds/White Pearls* and *The Last Seed*. He is working on his third book *Society's Child*, which deals with inspiring others to never give up on life despite common obstacles. He may be reached at 9505 Royal Lane, #2141, Dallas, TX 75243.

Sandra Keller appreciated the support from her family and friends while incarcerated, which enabled her to turn her life around and become a positive member of society. She can be reached at 4141 W. Pioneer Road, Mequon, WI 53097, e-mail: *skeller2000@yahoo.com*

Bob Kennington is a recovering addict and ex-offender who has worked in corrections for over twelve years and is instrumental in developing forty long-term, intense therapeutic communities in prisons in the U.S., Puerto Rico, France and Russia. He may be reached at 10 Burton Hills Blvd., Nashville, TN 37215; e-mail: *BobKennington@correctionscorp.com.*

Lucy Serna Killebrew is currently working on a mystery series. She has written a series of articles for *The Nashville Tennessean* about women who have used their incarceration to turn their lives around. She may be reached at #117005, MLRC, 6000 State Road, Memphis, TN 38134.

Brandon Lagana is senior assistant director of admissions at Ball State University. He was a volunteer at Gander Hill Prison in Delaware and active in many volunteer activities, including the Student Association of Volunteer Opportunities at West Chester University and Habitat for Humanity in Pennsylvania. He may be reached at the Office of Admissions, Ball State University, Muncie, IN 47306; e-mail: *blagana@juno.com*.

Laura Lagana, RN, is a registered nurse, professional speaker, member of the National Speakers Association and author of an upcoming inspirational book about nurses, patients and caregivers. She may be reached at Success Solutions, P.O. Box 7816, Wilmington, DE 19803-7816; e-mail: *NurseAngel@LauraLagana.com;* Web site: *http://www.LauraLagana.com*.

Dave LeFave is an inmate in the Colorado Department of Corrections. He was born and raised in Massachusetts and has spent most of his adult life in prison. He has written numerous poems. He may be reached at #86651, AVCF, Unit 4, P.O. Box 1000, Crowley, CO 81034.

Sid Madwed is a professional speaker, keynoter, author, consultant, engineer, lyricist, poet and seminar leader. He is a member of the National Speakers Association, the International Speakers Network and Poet Laureate of the New England Speakers Association. He may be reached at e-mail: *sid@madwed.com;* Web sites: *http://www.madwed.com/*.

James Malinchak is a contributing editor for *Chicken Soup for the College Soul,* a contributing author to *Chicken Soup for the Teenage Soul* and *Chicken Soup for the Kid's Soul,* and the author of five motivational books. He is a professional speaker who presents his motivational and inspirational talks over 150 times a year to business groups, college students and teenagers. He was named College Speaker of the Year by *Campus Activities* and a Consummate Speaker of the Year by *Sharing Ideas*.

Yitta Mandelbaum is the author of *Holy Brother: Inspiring Stories and Enchanted Tales about Rabbi Shlomo Carlebach,* in which her story originally appeared. She is also the coauthor of the national bestselling series *Small Miracles*.

Matt Matteo is an established artist, author of two widely published cartoon series, a book illustrator and adult tutor. A native of Derry, Pennsylvania, he often contributed his talent to benefit nonprofit groups and volunteers. He may be contacted at BS-7345, 801 Butler Pike, Mercer, PA 16137.

Nanci McGraw is a professional speaker, author, and award-winning broadcaster. She is called a "passionate communicator with creative, clear ideas" on organizing, communications, and achievement. She presents about 160 programs annually, and has presented in all fifty United States, as well as Canada, Hong Kong, Singapore, and Malaysia. She may be reached at P.O. Box 178424, San Diego, CA 92177-8424; e-mail: *nanci@mcgrawcom.com;* Web site: *http://www.nanci.org*.

John McPherson is a syndicated cartoonist and creator of *Close to Home*, a single-panel cartoon that appears in 650 newspapers worldwide, including the *Washington Post,* the *Los Angeles Times* and the *Tokyo Times.* He may be contacted at e-mail: *closetohome@compuserve.com;* Web site *www.closetohome.com.*

Felixa Miller was formerly employed in the defense industry. She is now semi-retired and lead by the Holy Spirit into active participation in the Catholic Church's Detention Ministry. Her experiences have brought greater understanding into the plight of a significant part of American society, who have, for the most part, been forgotten and neatly swept under the rug out of sight. She may be contacted at Felixa Miller, Our Lady of Grace Catholic Church, 5011 White Oak Ave., Encino, CA 91316-3799; e-mail: *felixa99@aol.com.*

Tekla Dennison Miller is a former warden of a men's maximum and a multi-level women's prisons in Michigan. She is a consultant, social activist, writer and national speaker focusing on women's issues, juvenile and criminal justice reform and the death penalty. Her memoir, *The Warden Wore Pink,* about her twenty-year career in corrections, is available and she can be contacted through Biddle Publishing Company, P.O. Box 1305, #103, Brunswick, ME 0401; e-mail: *tekla@frontier.net.*

Dan Millstein is the founding director of Visions for Prisons a nonprofit 501(c)(3) organization, and founder of the Peace in Prison2000 project. Along with his prison work he is a speaker and seminar leader, writer, visionary and consultant to businesses and individuals both in the Americas and Europe. He can be reached at P.O. Box 1631, Costa Mesa, CA 92628; 714-556-8000; Fax 714-546-FROG (3764); e-mail: *vfp95@aol.com;* Web site: *www.visionsforprisons.com.*

Christine Money is the warden of the Marion Correctional Institution, a two-thousand-bed medium-security prison in Marion, Ohio. She has worked for the Ohio Department of Rehabilitation and Correction for nineteen years. Warden Money has a masters degree in social work and has been a strong advocate for rehabilitative programs for inmates. She may be contacted at MCI, P.O. Box 57, Marion, OH 43302.

Ken "Duke" Monse'Broten, pen name Edward Allen Lee, is a grandfather originally from Park River, North Dakota. He has written numerous articles and short stories. He just completed a book, under his pen name, called *Messages of the Heart.* Reach him at #3571494 Snake River Correctional Institute, 777 Stanton Blvd., Ontario, OR 97914.

Rexford R. Moore Jr. is a geologist, serving a life sentence. He was a successful oil and gas producer for thirty-five years before being imprisoned. He may be reached at #149780, P.O. Box 260, Lexington, OK 73051-0260.

Nancy Muhammad is married to her best friend. She is a counselor and mentoring coordinator at a middle school. Mentoring is her passion. She believes that every child deserves a positive role model who will listen to them. She is especially concerned about children of incarcerated parents, an often-overlooked group. She may be contacted at e-mail: *nancyzmu@aol.com.*

Geraldine Nagy, Ph.D. is speaker and coauthor of *How to Raise Your Child's Emotional Intelligence: 101 Ways to Bring Out the Best in Your Children and Yourself.* Her doctoral degree is in psychology. She has spoken for organizations throughout the U.S. and South America. She may be reached at Heartfelt Publications, P.O. Box 1090, Bastrop, TX 78602, e-mail: *heartfelt@attglobal.net;* Web site: *www.heartfeltpublications.com.*

Robert C. Perks is president of Creative Motivation and author of the book *The Flight of a Lifetime.* He is a member of the National Speakers Association and a training consultant with the state of Pennsylvania. He may be reached at 88 North Pioneer Avenue, Shavertown, PA 18708-1024; Fax 570-696-1310, e-mail: *Bob@BobPerks.com;* Web site: *www.bobperks.com.*

Virginia Pool is the mother of a male Texas prisoner. She has two children and two grandchildren. She is a computer freak and spends a lot of time on the Internet. She's member of the Texas Inmate Families Association (TIFA). She may be contacted at e-mail: *Backfoot@aol.com;* Web site: *http//members.aol.com/footback/index.html.*

Sister Helen Prejean is a Catholic nun and author of the bestselling book, *Dead Man Walking.* She has befriended murder victims' families and helped found Survive, a victims' advocacy group in New Orleans.

Willie B. Raborn is married and has three children and six grandchildren. His stories appear in *Guideposts, Insight, Family Life Today, Good News* and others. He created and facilitated a rehabilitation program for repeat offenders called Foundations for Freedom. He's from Chatawa, MS, and is serving ten and a half years. He is a "student of freedom." He may be reached at P.O. Box 1054, Summit, MS 39666.

Mary Rachelski and her husband, Andy, have been involved in prison ministry since 1989. She volunteers several days a week in the Institute Activities Coordinator's office. The purpose is to introduce as many programs as possible to help the men help themselves. She and her husband teach self-esteem classes, and she holds a weekly Twelve-Step meeting. They are currently trying to get John Gray's *Men Are from Mars* materials into the correctional system and in the meantime facilitate workshops in their home in the St. Louis area to the public. She may be reached at Missouri Eastern Correctional Center, 18701 Old Highway 66, Pacific, MO 63069; e-mail: *jailbirdlady@hotmail.com.*

Kimberly Raymer is a romance author who has had three novels published by Kensington Publishing Corporation over the last year. Born and raised in Virginia, she has a B.A. in English from Christopher Newport College of the College of William and Mary, and is a member of the Romance Writers of America and of the Georgia Romance Writers. She and her husband presently live in Peachtree City, Georgia. She may be contacted on e-mail: *kimraymer@mindspring.com.*

Linda Reeves is the executive director of the Texas Inmate Families Association (TIFA). She serves on several Advisory Committees, including the Windham School District Title IV (Safe and Drug-Free Schools); and the Texas Department of Criminal Justice Family Advisory Committee. She currently chairs the Texas Youth Commission Prison Industry and Texas Youth Commission Education and Technology Advisory Committee and serves on the Board of the Crime Prevention Institute, Inc. She may be contacted at InFo, P.O. Box 788, Manchaca, TX 78652; 512-442-4637; e-mail: *infoinc@flash.net*; Web site: *www.inmatefamilies.org.*

John M. Reynolds is a penitent soul, serving time in the Missouri correctional system. He narrates educational texts onto audiocassette tapes for blind and disabled adults and children. He tutors GED and functionally illiterate men in Missouri prisons. He may be reached at #503608, Tipton Correctional Center, Osaga Ave., Tipton, MO 65081.

Marcia Reynolds chose freedom after turning twenty in jail. She then completed two masters degrees and worked her way up the corporate ladder. Currently, she is a coach, speaker, and author of *Being in the Zone* and also *Capture the Rapture.* Her company, Covisioning, provides leadership training and coaching for individuals, corporations and government agencies. She may be reached at P.O. Box 5012, Scottsdale, AZ 85261; e-mail: *Marcia@ covisioning.com., http://www.covisioning.com.*

Radames M. Rios, MPS, is a graduate of New York Theological Seminary and a former prisoner. He has a vast experience presenting Conflict Resolutions Seminars (Alternatives to Violence Project), and has dedicated his life to making a difference with former prisoners as an AIDS/HIV educator. He may be reached at 591 Vanderbilt Ave., PMB #130, Brooklyn, NY 11238; e-mail: *RadamesRios@hotmail.com.*

Mike Robinson is a member of All Saint Lutheran Church in Novato, CA. He is a member of a six-person team that regularly provides spiritual contact with those residents in the San Quentin Hospital who cannot attend service in the San Quentin Chapel. He may be reached at P.O. Box 3102, Rohnert Park, CA 94927; e-mail: *MRobins1@prodigy.net.*

Kevin Scott Rodriguez is an ex-offender and past president of Walking Tall Toastmasters and winner of many speech contests. While in prison he was a Pre-Release Instructor in Wilmington, Delaware. Today he is a successful entrepreneur. He may be reached at P.O. Box 2841, Wilmington, DE 19805; e-mail: *Kevsrod@aol.com.*

George M. Roth is an inspirational writer and motivational speaker. He presents dynamic seminars and keynote speeches with a special emphasis on acquiring new perspectives. He is author of Sometimes Life Just Isn't Fair and is a member of the National Speakers Association, Screen Actors Guild and the American Federation of Television & Radio Artists. He may be reached at e-mail: *George@GeorgeRoth.com*; Web site: *http://www.GeorgeRoth.com.*

A. Douglas Rowley is an institutional activities coordinator at the Missouri Eastern Correctional Center. He is most proud of the programs and activities that he helps organize. He oversees for the Missouri Department of Corrections for the offender population. He may be reached at 18701 Old Highway 66, Pacific, MO 63069.

Michael G. Santos is serving a forty-five-year sentence in federal prison. He is a nonviolent drug offender struggling to prepare himself for the future. He may be reached at 2305 NW 100th St., Seattle, WA 98177. Web site: *http://www.halcyon.com/garyt/freedom/*.

David Smith served twenty years in federal prison. He is now a speaker, workshop developer, author and founder of New Directions in Corrections (NDIC). He offers viable, cost-effective and proven alternatives to our traditional correctional methods. Contact David or NDIC at P.O. Box 152139, Austin, TX 78715; e-mail: *davidsm124@cs.com;* Web site: *www.c-cubed.org.*

Christian Snyder is currently serving a five- to fifteen-year sentence in New York State. He launched a career in freelance cartooning while incarcerated four years ago. He has been published in numerous magazines and trade journals. Cartooning has been a positive rehabilitative tool for him, and he plans to pursue freelance cartooning as a full-time career upon his release.

Dick Swan is a priest of the Episcopal Church and a chaplain at the Marion Correctional Facility in Marion, OH. He has a business degree from the University of Cincinnati and an MBA from the University of Dayton. He and his wife, Mary Ann (Marv), have two grown daughters. He may be contacted at MCI, P.O. Box 57, Marion, OH 43301-0057; 740-382-5781 ext. 2346; fax 740-387-8736; e-mail: *mdswan@midohio.net.*

R. L. Todd is a native of Webster County, Missouri. He was widowed in 1987. He has five children and six grandchildren. He finds writing relaxing and a great way to share those deepest feelings most difficult to speak. Roger writes country, heart and soul, and gospel songs. He also writes custom poems for people who send him the names and occasion. He may be reached at 790 County Rd., 800 N. #7, Tolono, IL 61880.

Lou Torok was a prisoner in Kentucky. He was born in 1927 to Hungarian immigrants and orphaned at eleven days of age. He served honorably in the U.S. Navy in World War II. Torok authored four books, three plays, a screenplay, and hundreds of magazine and newspaper articles. Sadly, Lou Torok passed away a few months before this book was published, in March of 2000.

Afshin Valinejad is a writer for the Associated Press.

Gail Valla is the records supervisor at Plummer Community Corrections Center in Wilmington, DE. The Center is responsible for community-based work-release, inpatient drug/alcohol, house arrest and intensive probation. She is the recipient of various warden awards, bureau commendations, and the 1996 Community Corrections Director's Award. Birthday cards may be sent to Dr. Cook at my office at 38 Todd Lane, Wilmington, DE 19802.

Nancy Waller enjoys various kinds of volunteer work, such as helping with Habitat for Humanity, building churches, the Angel Tree Ministry and tutoring adults to read. As a part of the Angel Tree Ministry, she plans to provide copies of *Chicken Soup for the Prisoner's Soul* to fifty-plus caregivers of prisoners' children next Christmas.

Tony H. Webb was educated in anthropology at the University of Utah. He is currently promoting his forthcoming book of unhinged verse/bizarre tales, *Pandora's Shadow*. $9.00/copy or the equivalent in postage stamps. Include a six-inch-by-nine-inch, self-addressed, stamped envelope ($.99 postage or IRCs). Send to Chandelier Books, P.O. Box 7610, Tacoma, WA 98406-0610.

Judi Weisbart is president of We Mean Business, a seminar company helping women to succeed personally, professionally and economically. Her passion is helping create a world of peace and social justice for all. Judi serves as an instructor and development director of Women's Economic Ventures, a nonprofit organization. She may be reached at e-mail: *judi@wemeanbiz.com*.

Marianne Williamson is an internationally acclaimed author and lecturer. She is the cofounder, along with Neale Donald Walsch, of the Global Renaissance Alliance. She is the bestselling author of *A Return to Love, Illuminata, The Healing of America* and *Enchanted Love.* To be included on her mailing list, send your name, address, fax, and e-mail to Marianne Williamson c/o Hay House, Inc., 2776 Loker Ave. W, Carlsbad, CA 92008. Visit her Web site at: *www.marianne.com*.

G. Ashanti Witherspoon was raised in Chicago, IL, and was confined in Angola Prison for twenty-seven and a half years. He was the president of the CPR Team, Instructor/Trainer for the American Heart Association, a paralegal for the Law Library, member of the Episcopal Church, Kairos Prison Ministry, and is an author and motivational speaker. He may be reached at P.O. Box 902, Baton Rouge, LA 70821; Web site: *www.witherspoonenterprise.com*.

Judy Worthen is a Life Skills teacher at Maricopa County Juvenile Detention Center in Mesa, Arizona. She and her husband, Lee, have seven children and nine grandchildren (so far). Judy is a motivational speaker whose messages center around accentuating the positive. She can be reached at Mesa Detention Center School, 1810 S. Lewis Street, Mesa, AZ 85210; e-mail: *worthen@deseretonline.com*.

Permissions

We would like to acknowledge the following publishers and individuals for permission to reprint the following material. (Note: The stories that were penned anonymously, that are public domain, or that were written by Jack Canfield, Mark Victor Hansen, and Tom Lagana are not included in this listing.)

Even the Strong Have a Soft Spot. Reprinted by permission of Robert Fuentes. ©1997 Robert Fuentes.

The Sunray Catcher. Reprinted by permission of Ken "Duke" Monse'Broten. ©1996 Ken "Duke" Monse'Broten.

Light Came and Went and Came Again. Reprinted by permission of Willie B. Raborn. ©1997 Willie B. Raborn.

Being a "Souper" Parent. Reprinted by permission of Thomas Ann Hines. ©1999 Thomas Ann Hines.

A Convict's Letter to His Son. Reprinted by permission of Lou Torok. ©1998 Lou Torok.

Beautiful Music. Reprinted by permission of Kimberly Raymer. ©1999 Kimberly Raymer.

Mom's Final Act. Reprinted by permission of R. L. Todd. ©1997 R. L. Todd.

The Promised Visit. Reprinted by permission of Ron Ambrosia. ©1999 Ron Ambrosia.

Unsung "Sheroes." Reprinted by permission of George Castillo. ©1996 George Castillo. Excerpted from *My Life Between the Cross and the Bars*, G&M Publications. ©1996 G&M Publications, P.O. Box 657, Shalimar, FL 32579.

Putting on the Mask. Reprinted by permission of Linda Reeves. ©1999 Linda Reeves.

Where There's Faith. Reprinted by permission of G. Ashanti Witherspoon. ©1998 G. Ashanti Witherspoon.

Mail Call. Reprinted by permission of John M. Reynolds. ©1998 John M. Reynolds.

Envy. Reprinted by permission of Ken "Duke" Monse'Broten. ©1996 Ken "Duke" Monse'Broten.

Just a Touch. Reprinted by permission of Ken "Duke" Monse'Broten. ©1996 Ken "Duke" Monse'Broten.

A Father's Prayer. Reprinted by permission of John Gillette. ©1998 John Gillette.

Bringing the Outside to the Inside. Reprinted by permission of Christine Money. ©1999 Christine Money.

My Best Friend Jack. Reprinted by permission of George M. Roth. ©1998 George M. Roth.

Chicken Soup for the Soul

Improving Your Life Every Day

Real people sharing real stories — for nineteen years. Now, Chicken Soup for the Soul has gone beyond the bookstore to become a world leader in life improvement. Through books, movies, DVDs, online resources and other partnerships, we bring hope, courage, inspiration and love to hundreds of millions of people around the world. Chicken Soup for the Soul's writers and readers belong to a one-of-a-kind global community, sharing advice, support, guidance, comfort, and knowledge.

Chicken Soup for the Soul stories have been translated into more than 40 languages and can be found in more than one hundred countries. Every day, millions of people experience a Chicken Soup for the Soul story in a book, magazine, newspaper or online. As we share our life experiences through these stories, we offer hope, comfort and inspiration to one another. The stories travel from person to person, and from country to country, helping to improve lives everywhere.

Chicken Soup for the Soul.

Share with Us

We all have had Chicken Soup for the Soul moments in our lives. If you would like to share your story or poem with millions of people around the world, go to chicken-soup.com and click on "Submit Your Story." You may be able to help another reader, and become a published author at the same time. Some of our past contributors have launched writing and speaking careers from the publication of their stories in our books!

Our submission volume has been increasing steadily — the quality and quantity of your submissions has been fabulous. We only accept story submissions via our website. They are no longer accepted via mail or fax.

To contact us regarding other matters, please send us an e-mail through webmaster@chickensoupforthesoul.com, or fax or write us at:

Chicken Soup for the Soul
P.O. Box 700
Cos Cob, CT 06807-0700
Fax: 203-861-7194

One more note from your friends at Chicken Soup for the Soul: Occasionally, we receive an unsolicited book manuscript from one of our readers, and we would like to respectfully inform you that we do not accept unsolicited manuscripts and we must discard the ones that appear.

Chicken Soup for the **Soul**®

Tough Times, Tough People

TOUGH TIMES
WON'T LAST
BUT
TOUGH PEOPLE
WILL

101 Stories about
Overcoming the
Economic Crisis and
Other Challenges

Jack Canfield,
Mark Victor Hansen
& Amy Newmark

Tough times won't last, but tough people will. Many people have lost money, jobs and/or homes, or made cutbacks. Others have faced life-changing natural disasters, or health and family diffi culties. These en-couraging and inspirational stories are all about over-coming adversity, pulling together, and fi nding joy in a simpler life. Stories address downsizing, resolving debt, managing chronic illness, having faith, fi nding new perspectives, and blessings in disguise.

978-1-935096-35-1

Chicken Soup
for the Soul

Think
Positive

101 Inspirational
Stories about
Counting Your Blessings and
Having a Positive Attitude

Jack Canfield,
Mark Victor Hansen & Amy Newmark
Foreword by Deborah Norville

Every cloud has a silver lining. Readers will be inspired
by these 101 real-life stories from people just like them,
taking a positive attitude to the ups and downs of life, and
remembering to be grateful and count their blessings.
This book continues Chicken Soup for the Soul's focus on
inspiration and hope, and its stories of optimism and faith
will encourage readers to stay positive during challenging
times and in their everyday lives.

978-1-935096-56-6

Chicken Soup for the Soul®

for the

Answered Prayers

101 Stories of Hope,
Miracles, Faith,
Divine Intervention,
and the Power of Prayer

Jack Canfield,
Mark Victor Hansen,
and LeAnn Thieman

We all need help from time to time, and these 101 true stories of answered prayers show a higher power at work in our lives. Regular people share their personal, touching stories of God's Divine intervention, healing power, and communication. Filled with stories about the power of prayer, miracles, and hope, this book will inspire anyone looking to boost his or her faith and read some amazing stories.

978-1-935096-76-4

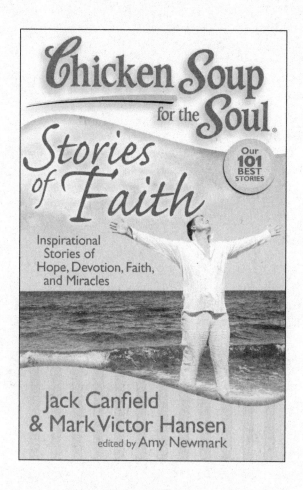

Chicken Soup for the Soul
for the Soul

Stories of Faith

Inspirational
Stories of
Hope, Devotion, Faith,
and Miracles

Our
101
BEST
STORIES

Jack Canfield
& Mark Victor Hansen
edited by Amy Newmark

Everyone needs some faith and hope! This book is just
the ticket, with a collection of 101 of the best stories from
Chicken Soup for the Soul's past on faith, hope, miracles,
and devotion. These true stories, written by regular people, tell of prayers answered miraculously, amazing coincidences, rediscovered faith, and the se-renity that comes
from believing in a greater power, ap-pealing to
Christians and those of other faiths — any-one who seeks
inspiration.

978-1-935096-14-6

Chicken Soup for the Soul

www.chickensoup.com